EARLY HISTORY OF AMENIA

By Newton Reed

with

Impressions of Amenia

By Dewey Barry

Epigraph Books
Rhinebeck, NY

Fifth Edition
Published 2012

First Edition
Delacey & Wiley, Amenia 1875

Second Edition
The Harlem Valley Times, Inc. Amenia 1964

Third Edition
The Harlem Valley Times, Inc. Amenia 1976

Fourth Edition
The Harlem Valley Times, Inc. Amenia 1985

Early History Of Amenia © 2012 By Newton Reed

Printed in the United States of America

Book and cover design by Barbara Patterson

ISBN 978-1-9369403-5-6
Library of Congress Control Number: 2012939533

PUBLISHER'S NOTES

Second Edition 🌿

As publisher of the Harlem Valley Times, it has long been my desire to republish the famous "Early History of Amenia" by Newton Reed. There were few copies of the original edition left, and I felt this little volume contained much that was extremely informative about this community's early beginnings.

With the introduction of new press equipment in the newspaper plant in January, that desire became practical. Under the guidance of James Brandt, foreman, and with Warren Harvey at the keyboard of the Intertype, the book became a reality.

We hope you enjoy this little volume.

Elliott McEldowney, Publisher
Amenia, N.Y.
March 3, 1964

Third Edition 🌿

It is with great pride we publish the third edition of "Early History of Amenia" by Newton Reed. This is the 100th anniversary of the history, the first copies being issued in 1875.

This small volume sets something of a record in continuous community interest.

We are also grateful we were able to republish this book in time for America's bicentennial.

Elliott McEldowney, Publisher
The Harlem Valley Times
Amenia, N.Y.
December 1975

Fourth Edition 🌿

It is with considerable pride we publish the fourth edition of "Early History of Amenia" by Newton Reed. This new edition contains the most recently published "Impressions of Amenia" by Dewey Barry.

This small volume sets something of a record in continuous community interest.

Elliott McEldowney, Publisher
Harlem Valley Times
Amenia, N.Y.
April 1985

PREFACE TO FIFTH EDITION

When Newton Reed completed *Early History of Amenia* in 1875, he created a legacy for future generations of Amenia citizens, a bequest of historical facts regarding the settlement of Amenia during the eighteenth century. His book is a treasure chest of cherished knowledge about Amenia families and individuals, their hamlets, industries and institutions.

The decade following the Civil War was bustling with railroad travel and westward expansion. Amenia's population had shifted dramatically, due to almost thirty years of Irish immigration, the rapid growth of the iron mining industry, and a booming dairy industry. Newton Reed ignored those historic events in order to focus on gathering information about the early settlers, information which had never been written down, which could not be found in other books, newspapers, or records, and which was in danger of being lost forever.

A century later, when Dewey Barry, grandson of an Irish immigrant, wrote his collected essays, "Impressions of Amenia," he was expanding upon and highlighting earlier information, as well as, capturing stories of historical interest, which he desired to document as part of the larger body of Amenia history.

Both of these authors have done a great service to our community by faithfully researching and recording Amenia's heritage. In reprinting their work, it is hoped that another generation of Amenia residents will appreciate and preserve this legacy.

In this Fifth Edition, the attempt has been made to carefully reproduce the original work of the authors, with a few corrections in the alphabetization of names and some minor changes in punctuation. This edition is illustrated with vintage photographs and maps from 1876, which should be of use in locating places referred to in the text. We have also added a list of recent publications related to Amenia history.

Elizabeth C. Strauss
Amenia Historical Society
Amenia, NY
2012

ACKNOWLEDGEMENTS

I would like to express my appreciation to the Amenia Historical Society, its members and Board of Trustees, for their support in this endeavor to preserve and promote Amenia's history.

Thanks to Ann Linden for her keen eye and voice of experience.

To those who have assisted in providing illustrations, David Reagon, our cover photographer, Robert Riemer, Ducillo Construction, the Sharon Historical Society archives, and the Amenia Historical Society archives, a hearty thanks, as well.

Gary Thompson deserves our praise and gratitude for his many hours of labor in preparing more than half of the images for this book. From his home in New Mexico, he has generously given of his time and expertise.

Certainly, a special word of thanks is due to Lauren and to Barbara at Epigraph, who have labored with great skill and sound advice, to make this book come to fruition, and to Maureen and Paul at Epigraph for their assistance and encouragement, as well.

For more information regarding the photo archives, maps and genealogy contained in this book, please contact the Amenia Historical Society by visiting http://ameniany.gov.

E.C.S.
2012

Newton Reed (1805 – 1896) *AHS*

NEWTON REED

1805 – 1896

Newton Reed was the grandson of an Amenia settler, Eliakim Reed of Norwalk, CT. His parents were Ezra and Esther (Edgerton) Reed. Newton lived his entire life on the family farm, about a mile south of Amenia Union. He was the eighth of Ezra Reed's eleven children.

Newton Reed was a naturalist. He knew the streams and valleys, the trees and crops, and the Indian lore of the area. His intense interest in the natural history of the region led him to become the primary authority on early traditions, paths, boundaries and settlements.

Reed was a historian and, hence, a writer and lecturer on local history. He gathered information about the families who came from New England, as well as about those people who came to Amenia a few decades earlier, the Dutch, the Palatine Germans, and the French Huguenots.

Reed was well versed in the history of Dutchess County, of nearby Connecticut, and of his beloved Oblong Valley. He had connections with the past through those Revolutionary War veterans he knew as a young man, and through his neighbors and friends who were barely a generation or two removed from the early settlers identified in *Early History of Amenia*.

Highly esteemed as a writer, Reed contributed to several journals of his day, *Country Gentleman*, *New York Observer*, and *Amenia Times*. Simply an "R." at the end of an article let readers know that it was from the pen of Newton Reed.

As an "agriculturalist," Reed researched, experimented and commented upon methods of husbandry. He also wrote articles on political and social matters, and on theology and religion.

That Reed wrote about theology is not surprising, since from his youth he had planned to go into the ministry, rather than farming. He became an elder in the South Amenia Presbyterian Church when he was twenty years of age, and served in that capacity for 70 years. He often lectured from the pulpit.

Newton and Ann (Van Dyck) Reed had a family of eight children. Their son Albert died in the Civil War. After Newton's death, his son Henry took over the family farm. Henry Van Dyck Reed followed his father as an elder in the church.

As an example of good character and intellect, Newton Reed was a man of influence in his community, respected for his astute observations and sound judgment. Amenia has had several great men in its history, but Newton Reed stands out as one of the most admirable.

E.C.S. 2012

INDEX

The names of the Early Residents and of the subscribers to the Roll of Honor are placed in alphabetical order in the book and are therefore left out of the Index.

Chapter Headings in **BOLD** type.

INTRODUCTION

The history of a rural town not only gratifies a most reasonable curiosity, but possesses a positive value as a source from which is drawn the history of the State; and there is a peculiar importance belonging to the records of those towns, which had their beginning at the commencement of our national life. The people who laid the foundations of these small communities were laying the foundations of a great nation, and in no age or country has the character of a nation been so greatly formed by the people, in their primary associations. Any careful record of these communities will become more valuable as it grows older.

In making a memorial of the early settlers of Amenia, and of their first civil institutions, I purpose to present only those things worthy of record, which would soon be out of reach of any historical research, and without attempting to bring the record down to the present time, either of the events of general interest or of particular families.

There is no need, in such a work, of describing those physical features of the country, which remain unchanged, nor of introducing any part of general history, which may be found in books accessible to the ordinary reader.

Those in whose interest this work is undertaken need not be told that the sources of information are very unfruitful. There is a surprising absence of any written memorials of those families, which were the earliest here. They were men of toil, and not literary, or disposed to keep a record of their uneventful lives; and their secluded location was so far removed from any scenes of historic interest that these memorials, — which hardly come up to the dignity of history — will be of interest to only a few, besides the residents here and descendants of the earlier inhabitants.

The difficulty of finding exact data, and the desire to be as accurate as possible, and to be brief are the reasons why so much time and research should be necessary for so small a work. The writer expects to be reminded of some errors, and of the many unavoidable omissions.

GEOGRAPHICAL LIMITS

The Precinct of Amenia was to consist of the nine easternmost tier of lots of the Lower or Great Nine Partners, and of that part of the Oblong, lying between these lots and the Connecticut line. This included the present town of Northeast, south of a line running through the northern part of the village of Millerton. The town of Amenia, when organized, had the same geographical limits.

NINE PARTNERS

The Great Nine Partners Patent was granted in 1697 to Caleb Heathcote, and others, and it covered the territory very nearly, which is now included in the towns of Clinton, Pleasant Valley, Washington, Stanford, Amenia, except the Oblong, and the south part of Northeast, except the Oblong. This grant was made before the Oblong was ceded to New York, and was bounded east by what was then the colony line.

This patent was divided into thirty-six principal lots, besides nine narrow water lots, which extended to the Hudson River, across the southern part of the town of Hyde Park, and the "nine easternmost lots," Nos. 28 to 36, were allotted one to each of the nine proprietors. The south lot in the tier, No. 28, was allotted to Augustus Graham, No. 29 to John Aretson, No. 30 to Henry Filkin, No. 31 to Caleb Heathcote, No. 32 to James Emmott, 33 to William Creed, 34 to David Jamison, 35 to James Marshall, and 36 to Hendrick Ten Eyck. The lots were nearly equal, containing about 3,400 acres, varying somewhat according to the quality of the land.

The Little Nine Partners tract was north of this and corresponded nearly with the towns of Milan, Pine Plains, and the northwest part of Northeast. This patent was granted to Sampson Boughton and others in 1706.

"THE OBLONG"

"The Oblong," or "Equivalent Land," was ceded to New York by Connecticut, after years of controversy, in 1731 — 61,440 acres — was 580 rods in width, and was divided into two tiers of square lots, called 500 acres each, though exceeding that. It was sold, by the colonial government of New York, to Hawley & Co., and allotments made to the individuals of the Company, and by them sold to emigrants, "who received a guarantee of title from the colonial government." "It was this security of title, which caused these lots to be eagerly sought after by emigrants." The Crown also gave a deed of the lands to an English company, which endeavored to maintain its claim in the English court of chancery, and the suit was brought to an end only by the Revolutionary war.

This land was surveyed and divided by Cadwallader Colden, Surveyor-General and Lieutenant Governor of New York, who was one of the Commissioners. Another of the Commissioners was Gilbert Willett. They became owners of some of the land. The Oblong lots included in Amenia were numbers 43 to 72.

The name "Oblong," -- at first applied to the whole tract — became after a few years limited to that valley in Amenia, of six or seven miles in extent, now Amenia Union and South Amenia.

The history of this controversy is this. In 1664, it was agreed between the two colonies that the boundary line should run from a certain point on Long Island Sound north-northwest to the Massachusetts line; both parties then understanding that this line would be parallel to the Hudson River, and twenty miles from it, which was the acknowledged limit of the two colonies. This was when the whole country north of Long Island Sound was an unknown land, and there was a great misconception of the points of the compass; for this direction would lead to the Hudson River below West Point.

When this error, which both parties recognized, was made apparent, it was agreed to rectify it. But the people who had settled on lands defined by that boundary very earnestly desired to retain their civil connections with the Connecticut colony; it was therefore agreed by that colony to cede to New York an equivalent in territorial extent, equal to the present towns of Greenwich, Stamford, New Canaan, and Darien, an area 12 miles by 8 -- 61,440 acres.

The agreement was completed and subscribed by the Commissioners at Dover[1] on the 14th of May 1731, after the entire survey had been made by them, and the monuments set up.

The survey was made, by running a random line from a given point to the Massachusetts' boundary, and the true boundary between New York and Connecticut was found by perpendicular surveys from this random line. This accounts for the fact that the monuments, which mark the boundary line between the two states, are not in a true line, which has excited a vexatious controversy for so many years and is not even yet settled.[2]

1   Dover is spoken of by the Commissioners in their report as a village, the only one on the west side of the Oblong; and Ridgefield and New Milford the only villages on the east side.

2   The Governor of Connecticut, in his recent message, called the attention of the Legislature to this subject.

ASPECT OF THE COUNTRY

There was not an unbroken forest here when the first settlers came; as fires of the Indians, in their pursuit of game, had destroyed the timber on the dry lands, except a few isolated specimens of oak, white wood, and wild cherry, some of which attained great size. On the plains there were scattered small oaks, which had sprung up after the fires, and by the creeks, and in the wetlands, there were large button-wood and black-ash trees; and all the streams were overhung with a mass of alders and willows. The mountains, it has been said, were covered with a less dense growth of wood than at present. It is evident that, in the valleys, the white wood, or tulip tree, and the wild cherry have given place to other trees, as the elm; and that on the mountains, the chestnut has greatly increased. The mountains, being burned over also by the Indians, were so bare that the wild deer were plainly seen from the valleys below.

There were but a few of the large wild animals; only a few deer, and an occasional otter in the creeks; and very rarely a wolf.

The principal stream, called in Dover, the "Ten Mile River," and in Amenia, the "Oblong River," was called by the Indians the Weebutook,[3] and its largest tributary from the west in this town was called by them the "Wassaic."[4] These streams were stocked with herring, and were frequented by great numbers of minks, and were the resort and breeding place of wild ducks.

---

3   Weebutook signified "Beautiful Hunting Ground." This is the interpretation given by Eunice Mauwee, granddaughter of the Chief, Gideon Mauwee, of the Scatacook tribe of Indians in Kent, Conn. It was she who attained the age of 102 years.

4   The Indians' word Wassaic is understood to signify "Difficult," or requiring hard labor, perhaps on account of the difficulty of access to the stream in its rocky chasm. In 1703, it was written "Washaick." The village of Wassaic was so called in 1843.

THE INDIANS

When the first settlers came, they found several scattered remnants of the Pequot Indians,[5] who had their hunting grounds up and down these valleys. They had a village in the northeast part of town, on the west side of Indian Pond, called Wequagnoch, a settlement called Checomico, near Pine Plains, and at Scatacook, in Kent, Conn., there was a considerable tribe. There was constant intercourse between these different settlements, and frequent migrations from one to another.

The remarkable labors of the Moravian missionaries among these Indians began in 1740, and were attended with every evident success, but the missionaries were so annoyed, and their people, by the officers of the colonial government that in a very few years they were driven out of the state.[6] These worthy Christian laborers were charged with being Jesuits, and emissaries of the French, a most odious and unreasonable imputation.

It may be some palliation of this excessive jealousy, that the missionaries were foreigners, and that this was a period of our country's history when the French in Canada were sending their emissaries – especially the Jesuits – to the Indians on our northern borders to excite them against the English and the colonies; though there is no reason now to believe that the influence of these emissaries extended to the scattered and feeble bands of Indians in this part of the state. It should be noted also that it was not by the local authorities that the missionaries were disturbed, for they were held in high esteem by their English neighbors.[7]

There was not only no outbreak here between the Indians and the whites, but they lived in perfect friendship, and the rights of the Indians were faithfully guarded by the stronger and more sagacious party.

After the Christian Indians had been driven out by the state, the Scatacooks of Connecticut continued their annual excursions through the Valleys of Amenia till after the beginning of the present century, and until the last remnant of the tribe had sunk into idleness and intoxication.[8]

---

5   That they were Pequots is generally accepted on the authority of the accurate historian Trumbull.

6   These exiles went first to Bethlehem, Penn., under the friendly care of the Brethren, and thence to Canada.

7   A valuable and pleasing history of these Moravian missionaries was prepared by Rev. Sheldon Davis in 1858, the original manuscript journal of the missionaries having then recently been discovered in the historical archives of the Brethren at Bethlehem.

8   At a place by the river called the "Nook," near South Amenia, the Indians were accustomed to hold their noisy "pow-wows." There were a few Indian wigwams near the outlet of Swift's Pond.

After the dispersion of the Indians, one of the Moravian missionaries – Rev. Joseph Powell – ministered to the congregation of the early settlers at the station in Amenia, near Indian Pond, where he died in 1774. He was buried there, with some of his people, on the field of his labors, in the burying ground of the brethren, near their house of worship. Here also the monumental stone says James Alworth died, 1786, age 73, Mary Alworth died, 1797 (and others). This ground, consecrated by missionary and Christian burial, is on the farm of Col. Hiram Clark, in the present town of Northeast, not far east of his house and on the west side of Indian Pond.[9]

Rev. Abraham Reinke, another of the Moravian Brethren, ministered to the people, in different parts of the town, before the settlement of a pastor.

---

9   Several Indian burial places are spoken of in tradition: one on lands of Myron B. Benton; another where that old burying ground lies, near Amasa D. Coleman's, still the burial place of families in that vicinity. Besides these, it has often happened that bones, evidently of Indian remains, have been disinterred in the Oblong valley.

FIRST SETTLEMENTS

MR. SACKETT

Mr. Richard Sackett[10] was here several years before any other settlement was made, though the precise year when he brought his family is not known. The place now known as the "Steel Works," on the Wassaic creek and the Harlem Railroad, was the place where he made his settlement, which is said to have been previous to 1711. In the Colonial Records, we read: "March 11, 1703, Richard Sackett petitioned government for license to purchase (of the Indians) a tract of land in Dutchess county, east of Hudson's river, called Washaick."

"Oct. 20, 1703, License granted."

"Nov. 2, 1704, Patent to Richard Sackett & Co. for said land, containing about 7,500 acres, or thereabouts."

"April 10, 1706, Patent to Sampson Boughton & Co. for a tract of land joining on the north side of above patent, and extending east to the colony line of Conn. and Waantinunk river, and north to the manor of Livingston."

Mr. Sackett was a resident of New York city, when he obtained the license and patent of 1703 and 1704. In 1711 and 1712, he was one of the commissioners with Mr. Robert Livingston, in settling the Palatines, at East Camp, or Germantown. This occupied so much of these two years, that he could not have spent much of his time at his new home in Washaick.

The patent of 1704 – "7,500 acres or thereabouts" – must have been covered by the Great Nine Partners' Grant, which was made May 27, 1697, making Mr. Sackett's subsequent title invalid.

The patent of April 10, 1706, to Sampson Boughton & Co., was that of the Little Nine Partners, and Mr. Sackett was one of the nine.

In 1726, Mr. Sackett made applications to the Connecticut Legislature for license to purchase of the Indians a tract of land in the west part of the town of Sharon. His petition was denied, though repeated several times.

He was never able to maintain his title to any of the Oblong lots, nor could his heirs, though his son – Dr. John Sackett – attempted in 1750, under the grant of 7,500 acres, to hold some of these lands against

---

10 He is called by tradition "Capt." Sackett, but in all the old public documents, he
    is mentioned as "Mr." Sackett.

Lieut. Gov. Colden and others.[11] Mr. Sackett died in 1746 and was buried on the hill, not far from his place of residence, in a little cemetery, now greatly neglected. There is no stone to mark his grave. [12]

He had three sons and two daughters.[13] To his son, Dr. John Sackett, he gave, by his will, the homestead, orchard,[14] and meadows, and improved lands, and also his books.[15] To his son Richard, he gave two hundred acres of land, above his equal share, "as being his eldest son." These bequests of land show Mr. Sackett's own estimate of his titles, some of which, at least, proved to be empty.

It may be supposed that Mr. Sackett, being much associated with Mr. Livingston, and observing his success in acquiring a large landed estate, was encouraged to enter upon a similar course. There is nothing, however, in the history of these traditions that appears unworthy of an honorable man. Gov. Hunter, in 1712, — to the Home Government — commends Mr. Sackett's "diligence and industry," and says, "and he well deserves a reward, to which I humbly recommend him."

At the time Mr. Sackett established his family in Amenia, there was not another white family in the county nearer than Poughkeepsie, and the whole population of Dutchess county, then including Putnam, was only 450. There was no settlement in the adjoining county of Litchfield, in Connecticut, except in Woodbury and New Milford.[16]

---

11 Lot No. 45 of the Oblong, which was near Mr. Sackett's place, was allotted to Gov. Colden, who made the survey of the Oblong, and was given by him to his son, Alexander Colden, who, in 1750, resurveyed Lots 43, 44, 45, and 46.
12 Barnabas Paine, Esq., says in his manuscript that he had several times visited the grave of Mr. Sackett in that place, but no stone can be found there which identified the grave.
13 The children of Mr. Sackett were Richard, John, Josiah Crego, Mary and Catherine. The last of the family that left here, grandsons of Mr. Sackett, went to Rennselaer Co.
14 The orchard was celebrated long after. One tree is left.
15 These books, some of which were on subjects of National History, show the literary disposition of the family. They were presented by Dr. John Sackett to Dr. Reuben Allerton, and after his death they were taken by his son, Dr. Cornelius Allerton.
16 There were twelve families in New Milford in 1712.

THE WINEGARS

In 1724, Capt. Garrett Winegar came to Amenia Union from East Camp, now Germantown, in Columbia county, on the Hudson river. His father Uldrick Winegar, then seventy-two years old, came with him. They were of those Palatines, who were forced out, destitute, from their native country, in the interior of Germany, out of revenge by Louis XIV, and were befriended by the English government, which gave them lands in this new country, and for some time a free subsistence. "The Elector Palatine, the head of the little state, having deserted the cause of France, orders were given to lay waste his country. The cruel edict was fearfully executed; two cities and twenty-five villages were reduced to ashes, and their innocent inhabitants were left to perish by cold and hunger."

A part of these people, brought to America by the friendly ships of Great Britain, were placed at the Camp, where six thousand acres of land were divided to their several families, and they were supplied also by the royal bounty of Queen Anne.[17] with present subsistence, with horses and cattle, and all those implements which are necessary for successful prosecution of their future industries. It was expected that there would be some return to the government for the favors in the production by the colonists of naval stores, hemp, tar, pitch, and pine lumber.

The six thousand acres, now the town of Germantown, was part of the manor of Livingston, and was released to the Crown by Mr. Livingston for this purpose, that it might be the home of these refugees. Many Palatines were located in other parts of the state.[18]

This settlement was made in 1710; and in 1724, Mr. Winegar, probably through some discontent, was led to seek a home in this unoccupied region. The cause of the discontent was this. The colonists complained of unreasonable exaction upon their productive industry, and the royal bounty of food was unjustly withheld from them by the commissioners, some of whom seem to have made too great a profit out of these subsidies.

It is a reasonable conjecture that Mr. Winegar's acquaintance with Mr. Sackett at the Camp may have led him to come to Amenia, and it

---

17 One of the royal gifts from Queen Anne was a church for their worship.
18 The Upper Palatinate was a small state lying on both sides of the Rhine, having Manheim for its capital. In 1674, the whole of it was rendered almost desolate by the troops of Louis XIV, who had no better motive than that the invaded province was a part of the empire with which he was then at war, and next, that the inhabitants were almost all Protestants. About 2,700 Palatines, who had sought refuge in England, were sent to America by the British government in 1710. They were mostly German Reformed or Presbyterian.

is evident that he was actuated by a spirit of independence and enterprise, and not by any desire for speculation.

He entered upon land at Amenia Union – where he built his house – without any title, except from the Indians, and afterwards, when the Oblong was confirmed to New York, and surveyed, he received a title from the proprietor of those lots at a reasonable price.

In 1739, Mr. Winegar purchased of Daniel Jackson 300 or 400 acres of land in Connecticut, adjoining his own, and removed into the house built by Jackson on the hill above the site of the brick factory, thus becoming a citizen of the town of Sharon. He had built a mill above the present mill sites of the place, which was the first mill in this part of the county, and the first building erected in the town of Sharon.

The character of Mr. Winegar for honesty was proverbial. He lived on the friendliest terms with the Indians, by whom he was regarded with the greatest respect, and whom he several times defended against the injustice of their white neighbors; and it is said that he gave his children charge at his death that they should never allow the Indians to go from their doors in want of food.

It is worthy of note that there is no mention of any block-house, or any defense against the Indians, put up by these early settlers, notwithstanding they were surrounded by large numbers of them, and were isolated for many years from any other white settlements; while in Litchfield, between 1720 and 1730, there were five houses surrounded by palisades, and soldiers were stationed there to guard the inhabitants while at work and at worship on the Sabbath.

Mr. Winegar died in 1755 in the midst of his enterprises. He made provision in his will for his fourteen children, and also made special and kind mention of his servant "Tom." His father, Uldrick Winegar, had died in 1754, aged 102 years. Their graves, and those of many of their descendants, are in that well-chosen burial place near Amenia Union.

Hendrick Winegar,[19] the oldest son of Capt. Garret, had his residence for many years at the foot of the west mountain, and in 1761 he built the large stone and brick house a short distance west of Amenia Union. He was the ancestor of the families of that name in Kent, Conn.

Uldrick, another son, was the grandfather of Capt. Samuel Snyder Winegar. Conrad Winegar, another son of Garrett, was a magistrate and public-spirited citizen in the town. His antique and quaint-looking old house, which stood near the rocks in rear of Samuel Hitchcock's house, remained till about 1820. His only son, Gerhard, or Garret, the grandfather of Garret H., was an officer in the Revolution, and died before the close of the war. Esq. Winegar held a valuable tract of land,

19   He was called Ensign Winegar.

extending from the highest point of the east mountain to that of the west. The wife of Capt. John Boyd and the wife of Col. Colbe Chamberlain were daughters of Esq. Winegar.

One of the daughters of Capt. Garrett Winegar was the wife of Nicholas Row, Sen. Another was the wife of Dr. Thomas Young, who will be mentioned again.Lieutenant Samuel Snyder, who was one of the Palatines, and came here with them, was the brother-in-law of Garrett Winegar, and his wife was the daughter of Henry Nase.

His house was where John D. Barnum lives. He was 95 years old when he died in 1808. Here is now (1875), planted by him, the first pear tree grown in this part of the land.

THE ROWS

The Rows were also Germans, and are supposed to have been also of the Palatines, and to have come to this place soon after the Winegars and previous to 1731. See old map of Nine Partners.

"Johannes Rouh died in 1768, aged 72 years." He lived where the brick house now stands built by Henry Morehouse. He was the father of Nicholas, Sen., and William. The sons of Nicholas, Sen., were Nicholas, Jun., Samuel, Conrad, and Garrett.[20] The sons of Nicholas, Jun., were William, Nicholas, John, Henry, Conrad, and Gilbert. His wife was the daughter of John Lovel. Of the other sons of Nicholas, Sen., Conrad lived where Walter Sherman does, and Garrett built the Hilliard house, a stone building where Shadrack Sherman's house now stands.

The old houses, built by these early settlers, of which there were as many as seven or eight near Amenia Union, at the beginning of the present century, were objects of special interest.

There is a pen and ink map,[21] executed previous to 1731, of the Nine Partners, which shows the dwellings in Amenia at that time. Mr. Sackett's is shown, and Henry Nase's, four near Amenia Union, and one on Lot 33. The Lot lines seem to be drawn according to survey, and the streams and ponds are laid down with a good deal of accuracy. The map is supposed to have been made by the family of one of the proprietors of the grant.

The dwelling on Lot 33 is probably intended for that of Salisbury, who is mentioned on page 33.

---

20 One of the daughters of Nicholas Row, Sen., was the wife of Benjamin Delamater. Another was the wife of Capt. William Young.

21 The compiler is indebted to Mrs. Caroline Germond, a descendant of Henry Filkin, one of the Nine Partners, for the use of this map.N.B. – Space would fail to mention all the voluntary contributions, which have been made to assist in this work.

The four houses near Amenia Union confirm the supposition that Mr. Row was there previous to 1731, and the location of one of the houses agrees with that of Mr. Row.

This steadfast Christian people have not gained that historical notice which has been acceded to the Huguenots and to the Hollanders; and it may be suggested as a reason that the Germans, at their early and enforced emigration, and out of their great poverty, neglected the higher education and were without a historian to make a memorial of their deeds.

HENRY NASE

In 1725, Henry Nase settled in the south part of the town. His memorial stone, in the cemetery at Dover, says: "Henry Nase, born in high Germany, died Dec. 14, 1759, about 64 years old." His residence was near where his grandson, Cornelius, lived, but on the opposite or east side of the river,[22] and here also his son Philip, Sen., resided, who was the father of Henry, John, Philip, Cornelius, and William. Henry, the oldest of these, being a tory, emigrated to Nova Scotia after the Revolutionary war. The others occupied four contiguous farms in that beautiful agricultural district.

KNICKERBACKER AND VANDUSEN

It appears that these families were in the south part of the town at an early period and also that Jacob Van Camp and Derrick Dutcher were in the north part of Dover, previous to 1731.[23]

There is a deed, written in Dutch, or Holland language, of the date of 1711, from Herman Knickerbacker to Cornelius Knickerbacker. It appears to be of land occupied by Van Dusen, and the house of Van Dusen was a short distance east of George T. Belding's.

It was about 1720 that Van Dusen, Knickerbacker and Dutcher purchased land in Salisbury of the Indians, supposing, as has been said, that their purchases were within the province of New York.

"The first highway from Salisbury was from Weatague through Lakeville, Ore Hill, Sharon Valley, Sackett's Farm to Dover," [24] showing the intercourse of these Dutch families.

---

22 The old map mentioned above indicates that Mr. Nase's first house was on the east side of the river, which is also the testimony of tradition.

23 The old map shows the houses of Jacob VanCamp and Derrick Dutcher near Plymouth Hill.

24 Historical Address of Hon. Samuel Church, of Salisbury, Conn., at the Centennial Anniversary of that town in 1841.

DELAMATERS

Capt. Isaac Delamater settled where Samuel Sherman lives previous to 1740. He came from Kingston, Ulster county, where the family had lived for several generations. His father was Jacob, and his grandfather was Claude, who came to America after 1645 and before 1650.

They were Huguenots, and like a large portion of that excellent people, made their escape from persecution[25] in France, first to Holland, and thence to America, and thus became identified in that country and in this with the Hollanders. It is a striking fact, and exemplified in the subsequent chapters of this history, that so many of the early settlers of Amenia were brought here by their love of freedom.

Capt. Delamater died April 20, 1775, the very day after the battle of Lexington,[26] and was buried in his own field. He was also a magistrate, and though many quaint things were said and done by this eccentric justice, his integrity and good sense were never questioned. It is an accredited tradition that in judicial cases of importance he consulted his wife, who sometimes sat by his side in court.

He had been a captain of a company of colonial troops in the French war, and took special interest in military affairs, calling the young men of his district together to his house for instruction in military art.

Capt. Delamater was a large landowner, and gave farms to his sons. Martin remained at the homestead. Benjamin built a stone house north of Horace Reed's. John (Honnes) built a mill at Leedsville – the first in the town — and also, in 1761, he built the brick house,[27] now the property of Myron B. Benton. Isaac, Jun., lived on the farm now owned by Newton Reed, where he built a house, which is now the oldest building in the town of Amenia. Mr. Delamater owned also the farm of Edward E. Cline. John Delamater, of Leedsville, was the grandfather of John Delamater, M.D., L.L.D., who was a distinguished physician and surgeon, and who was a professor in the medical institutions of Pittsfield, Mass., Fairfield, N.Y., and Cleveland, Ohio. He died in Cleveland in 1867.[28] There were several other physicians in the family.[29]

---

25 It is recorded in history that 200,000 French Protestants suffered martyrdom, and 700,000 were driven from the kingdom.

26 The house built by Mr. Delamater was brick and burned about 1819.

27 J.M.D. seen on face of the wall stands for John and Mary Delamater.

28 Dr. John Delamater's mother was Elizabeth Dorr, a descendant of William Hyde, of Norwich, Conn., and consequently is named in that remarkable genealogy, prepared by the late Chancellor Reuben Hyde Walworth.

29 Ex-Gov. Todd, of Ohio, is a descendant of John Delamater. Ex-President Colfax and Wm. M. Evarts are also members of this family.

Besides the families named above, all of whom emigrated from the North river, there was one Baltus Lot, who lived awhile in the north part of this town and on the public lands in the town of Sharon, and Adam Showerman is mentioned as being about the same time in that part of the town. These were supposed to have come also from near the Hudson River.

There were several Dutch families settled on the Housatonic in Salisbury previous to this, and before any settlements were made there by the New Englanders.

FIRST SETTLERS FROM NEW ENGLAND

The first important immigration to these new lands from other parts of New York and from New England was not till about 1740. The Nine Partners' land had been in market for some time and was sold at first in rather large tracts. The Oblong lots were brought into market in 1731 and attracted many immigrants from Connecticut and Massachusetts.

From 1740 to 1750, the immigration was evidently large, from the significant fact that about 1750 the population was sufficient to encourage the people to institute public worship in three different places.

In the journal of Abraham Reinke, one of the Moravian missionaries who preached at "Nine Partners and Oblong," in 1753, he says: "The people came here five years ago in expectation of bettering their fortunes by the purchase of cheap farms, and for the enjoyment of religious liberty."[30] This shows that by his estimate a considerable portion of the people came here about 1748. It also gives a significant intimation of the spirit of the people in their jealous regard for their religious rights. The opportunity to obtain fruitful lands at a moderate price was very attractive. The better lands were easily cleared and brought immediate returns. The title was assured, and the price was moderate.[31]

Among the earliest of the first settlers from New England were Hezekiah King and Abraham Paine. It was somewhat previous to 1740, as Mr. King died in 1740, and he had built a house a little west of Amenia Union, afterward called the "Karner House."

The house was built in the style prevailing in Connecticut at that time, high in front and very low in the rear. The timber was white wood, which indicated its early structure, as all the oldest houses were of that timber.[32]

---

30 There was not any subjugation of the church to the state, which these emigrants fled from, but they were jealous of the least interference of the spiritual with the temporal power, and their theory of the entire separation of church and state is now the theory of every part of the United States. The plan of union adopted by the first settlers of Massachusetts was expressed by Rev. Mr. Cotton in his letter to Lord Say and Seal. "It is better that the Commonwealth be fashioned at the setting forth of God's house, which is his church, than to accommodate the church frame with the civil state." These historic facts had so much connection with the settlement of Amenia that without some reference to them we shall misunderstand one of the essential elements in the social history of this people.

31 The price of new land then was a dollar and a half per acre. In 1760 it was about two dollars and a half per acre.

32 A large number of the first houses built by settlers were commodious structures, and of pleasing architectural appearance. There were but few log houses. The white wood was very suitable for building. The two-story house built by Jedidiah Bump was covered entirely with siding from one tree.

Abraham Paine of Canterbury settled in the northern part of town, as it is, and also Joshua Paine, Jehoshaphat Holmes, and Elisha Cleaveland. About 1740 Nathan Mead came from Horse Neck, or Greenwich, that hive of Meads, and purchased where the family are still in possession. Stephen Kinney from New Preston settled in 1740 near the Separate, so called, where his family is still represented. Elisha Adams was the first resident in that part of the town called Adams' Mills, and the first in the west part of Lot 32 of the Nine Partners.

Benjamin Hollister from Sharon settled in 1741 near Leedsville, where some of his family are in possession. Joel Gillett came to the Delavergne farm in 1742. Gardiner Gillett lived north of where Hiram Cooper's residence now is, and on a road now discontinued, Abner Gillett was here previous to 1748, probably as early as 1742. He owned the farm of Geo. D. James.

About 1742, Capt. Stephen Hopkins, of Hartford, Conn., purchased a tract of land about a mile north of the present village of Amenia, and including the land on which the Old Red Meeting House stood. He purchased the north half of Lot 32 of Nine Partners, and appears to have purchased the right of Isaac Vanernom who had bought of John Salisbury. "There had been some improvements made by Salisbury."[33] Stephen Hopkins' house was southwest of the old burying ground, and was reached in late years by a lane, and was the residence awhile of Henry Ingraham.

Thomas Wheeler came from Woodbury in 1749 to lands, which are now held by his descendants. Daniel and Job Porter came also that year. Simeon Dakin from near Boston removed to the north part of the town, about 1750, and also Bezaleel Rudd, and Spencer. Captain David Collin settled on the place now occupied by his great grandson. John Pennoyer, removed from Sharon in 1749 to Oblong lot, No. 62. In the northwest part of town Abraham Bockee, from New York, settled on land purchased by his father in 1699, two years after the purchase of the Nine Partners' tract – land now held by his descendant, Phenix Bockee. Elijah Kinne was on a farm north of the City. It was a little later than these dates that Isaac Smith and others immigrated to that part of the town.

In the southeast part of the town, some of the earliest settlers were Davis, Rowley, Bump, Cady, Knapp, Woolsey, Woolcott, Mitchell, Curtis, Lothrop, Judson, Delano, Doty, and others, of whom a part were known there only a few years. Those families from Connecticut and

---

33 The dwelling of Salisbury is shown on the old map mentioned on page 29, though the location is not perfectly exact, nor the name. This Salisbury was probably the one referred to in Judge Church's Historical Address. He was not a landowner there nor here.

the Cape, who became the permanent residents, the Barlows, Swifts, Chamberlains, Reeds, Clines, Hitchcocks, and others migrated to their new homes here in the years from 1755 to 1769.

Those, and the early settlers in the other parts of the town, will be noticed in a subsequent part of this work, and it will be more convenient for the compiler and for the reader to have the names of the families arranged in alphabetical order, rather than in the order of the date of their settlement.

The formative period of the town's history was an eventful epoch also in the history of the colony. The population of the colony was rapidly increasing. In 1746, the population of Dutchess county was 8,800 and in 1756, it was 14,148, and the population of the colony of New York was 96,765.

There was war between England and France, and great activity in the military service, and the men were trained by their service in the French war for that national struggle which was to come. There was also a great agitation of religious questions arising out of the revival of religion under the ministry of Edwards and others.

The Winegar House (built 1761 by Hendrick, grandson of Uldrick) *AHS*

Historic Marker near Winegar home site *AHS*

John & Mary Delamater House at Leedsville (built 1761)
(Sketch by Myron Benton, c. 1860, in *Troutbeck* by Chas Benton)

Union Mill near Leedsville, c. 1833 *AHS*

Hitchcock House and Corners (aka The Oblong, later Amenia Union) *AHS*

Amenia Union Sign re Dr. Thomas Young who named Amenia. *AHS*
(House in photo was formerly Lambert's Store, c. 1867)

Site of Red Meeting House (in foreground),
Amenia Burying Ground (at right)
House in photo was originally the Baptist Parsonage (built c. 1824) *AHS*

The 1st Presbyterian Church of Amenia (built 1867; first edifice was the
Red Meeting House, built in 1758) *GT*

RELIGIOUS SOCIETIES

It is evident that a large number of families besides these – whose names are given and the date of their immigration – had settled upon these lands, as early as 1750, as indicated in their institution of public worship by several congregations about this time.

They had come into this newly-opened territory without any concert, each family purchasing their land independently of the others, and without any previous or immediate arrangement for establishing civil or ecclesiastical organizations. In this they were unlike the communities in New England, which made their settlements under the regulations of an organized association, civil and religious. Those were a homogeneous people and set out at once with all the advantages of a common centre and unity in their social life.

The absence of this municipal unity in the case of these immigrants, and the want of any public records in the beginning, may readily account for he lack of exact dates in their history.

These immigrants, however, notwithstanding their isolation and diversity of origin, soon began to lay the foundations of their welfare when they set up the institutions of religion, and united in that form of christian fellowship, which indicated their love of freedom, and which was the model of the then future free institutions of our country.

The Republican form of ecclesiastical government, adopted by so many of the churches in America, was not patterned after the form of the civil government of this country, which is much more recent. It is consistent with the teachings of history to say that the adoption of a republican form of ecclesiastical government by the churches at the time of the Reformation in France, Switzerland, Holland, Scotland, and partly in England, prepared the people for choosing the same form of government for he State.

The germ of American liberty was in the Reformation.

THE RED MEETING HOUSE

The territory afterwards included in the town of Amenia, being geographically divided into three principal valleys, there were three congregations organized for public worship, and they were all of the same order, Presbyterian,[34] or Congregational. The oldest – so far as recorded – of these churches was organized near the centre of the town, when

---

34   The term "Presbyterian" was then often applied to a Congregational church.

in May, 1748, Abraham Paine[35] and Gardiner Gillett entered into covenant, "The Lord having thus begun to build his church here." In July 1749, "Sixteen souls more were gathered into church fellowship." They called the name of the church "Carmel, in the Nine Partners."

In 1750, June 14, Abraham Paine, Jun., "was set apart to the work of the ministry by solemn ordination, by laying on the hands of the Presbytery, and by the power of the Holy Ghost." The ecclesiastical form of all the church and the doctrines were agreeable to those in New England at that time, and the council, called for the installation of Mr. Paine, were from Connecticut. The day of the ordination was observed with solemn fasting.

Mr. Paine does not seem to have been educated in early life for the ministry, but was invested with the office to meet the immediate wants of a newly organized congregation. One of the council at his ordination was his father's brother, Rev. Solomon Paine,[36] an eminent minister of Canterbury, Conn.

This society was instituted at a time when in New England the churches were agitated by the fiery zeal of the "New Lights," or "Separatists," and Mr. Paine and a considerable portion of his church were affected with their notions, which led to some disagreement between them and the more conservative of the congregation.

The Separatists were earnest and conscientious, but sometimes uncharitable and censorious, and their discipline took cognizance of the thoughts of the heart, which were confessed to one another, and were the subject of censure and rebuke.[37]

The Separatists, or New Lights, differed from other Congregationalists, not in their doctrines, but in their claim to have obtained a new spiritual Light, and to have reached a higher spiritual Life. A spirit of uncharitableness was indulged, and they were accustomed to denounce ministers and others as Antinomian, and unregenerated, and when their views did not govern in the church, they were disposed to separate themselves from it. In their ecclesiastical government, the Separatists held to that independency which the Pilgrims contended for when they fled from England to Holland, previous to their coming

---

35 Mr. Paine speaks of himself as "Abraham Paine, son of Elisha Paine, of Canterbury, Conn." There is an account of these families in their alphabetical order.

36 Another brother of his father had been an eminent lawyer, and became a Separatist minister, and subjected himself for his irregularities in preaching to persecution.

37 The record of a council of the church of the Red Meeting House, at which several members were subjected to discipline for various offences, especially "for the indulgence of an Antinomian and party spirit," says "This solemn assembly continued from Wednesday morning in solemn fasting, lamentation, prayer and confession, from the rising of the morning till the stars appeared on Saturday night."

over to Plymouth.[38]

The differences between the Pilgrims and the Puritans, which existed at that time, had not died out in New England in 1740, and scarcely now.

They both held fast to the doctrine of the Thirty-Nine Articles. But the Puritans, hoping for the purifying of the English church, did not sever their connection with it till they left for their new home.

The Separatists were also restive under the subjection in New England of the church to the civil authority, and were prepared to give a high tone to their independency in their new home, and to assert the rights of individuals and the equality of all men.[39]

The house of worship – which was always known as the "Red Meeting House" – was built in 1758. The place where it stood is a triangle at the convergence of the highways, about a mile northeast of the village of Amenia, and near the burying ground. It was a building nearly square, two stories, with a gallery on three sides, and was seated with square pews.

This house was built[40] and afterwards repaired partly by contributions of those not strictly adherents of the Congregational polity, and was occupied harmoniously in later years by the Congregationalists, Baptists and Methodists.

In 1770, in June, (or July, according to Sedgwick's oratory), the celebrated Whitefield preached in the Red Meeting House to the crowds that followed him from all the country round.

Elder Elijah Wood, a Baptist, was the acceptable minister of the congregation several years.

In the early part of the present century, the three denominations gradually became separated, and each sustained a separate organization.

There is no record of a settled pastor after Mr. Paine for many years, but there appears to have been preaching, stated and occasional, and the ordinances were administered by pastors of other churches and

---

38 This is the time when they received the name of "Separatists."

39 One of the King's officers, in pursuit of a deserter here, in 1761, says of the people in Nine Partners that "they are levellers from principle." (Doc. Hist., III, 985.)

40 The number of those who contributed to the building was seventy-nine and the amount contributed was 350 pounds – 17-4 = $877.17. Of those who contributed to this work, these names will be recognized. Stephen Hopkins is first with the sum of 20 pounds. Joshua Paine, Elias Shevilear, and Benjamin Benedict gave each 13 pounds. Samuel King 9 pounds. Jedidiah Dewey and Roswell Hopkins, each 10 pounds. Other names are Robert Freeman, Abraham Paine, Jun., Joab Cook, Grover Buel, Jonathan Shepard, Jun., Samuel Shepard, Nathan Mead, Jun., Simeon Cook, John King, Tristam Brown, Noah Hopkins, Michael Hopkins, Ichabod Paine, Sen., Ichabod Paine, Jun., Weight Hopkins, Job Mead, Peter Shevilear, Barnabas Paine, Robert Willson, John Hindman, and John Brunson. Their paper is dated "Nine Partners. Feb. 6, 1758." The site for this edifice was presented by Capt. Stephen Hopkins, who also gave the first land for the Burying Ground.

stated supplies, and there were evidently a large number of excellent Christian men connected with this congregation.

There was much distraction at the time of the Revolutionary war, and afterwards some degree of dissension in drawing the lines between the adherents of this church and the other denominations.

In 1811 this church was connected with the Associated Presbytery of Westchester, and in 1815 with the Presbytery of North River.

In 1825, Rev. Joel Osborn became pastor of the church and gave to it his services one-third of the time, which indicates the feebleness to which it was reduced. From that period there has been a gradual improvement.

THE BAPTIST CHURCH

The Baptist Church in Amenia, at its organization in 1790, appears to have been composed partly of some from the old Congregational church and of others who had been educated in the Baptist system, and who had been members of the Baptist church in Northeast,[41]

"On the 5th of May 1790, three brethren related their experience and signed the covenant, and on the 12th and 19th three more brethren and several sisters united with them."[42] On the 2d of June they chose Reverend Elijah Wood for their minister, who, on the 27th of June, "administered the ordinance of the Lord's supper to them for the first time."

Mr. Wood had ministered to the Congregational church some years, and it does not appear that his new change of views and his uniting himself with this new organization sundered the fraternal relations with the brethren of the old church, or lessened their confidence in him. We find him invited by the Society's committee – Deacon Shevalier, a Baptist, and Deacon Hebard, a Congregationalist – to continue his ministrations. The jealousy and strife, which after this disturbed the two churches, is happily now almost forgotten.

Rev. Elijah Wood was a native of Norwich, Conn., and went in early life to Bennington, Vt., where he was licensed to preach in a Congregational church. From Bennington he came to Amenia before the

---

41 The Baptist church in Northeast, at Spencer's Corners, was instituted in 1751 by Elder Simon Dakin, who came from the vicinity of Boston, where he had suffered some annoyance for his religious principles. This was the second Baptist church organized in the colony of New York, and became one of the most important. It was sustained by the large and influential family of Winchells, farmers of enterprise and wealth.

42 The names of those who first constituted the church were James Palmer, David Allerton, Richard Shevalier, Reuben Hebbard, Jonathan Shepherd, Samuel Paine, Deborah Palmer, Jeanett Allerton, Elizabeth Holmes, Thankful Hebbard, and Mary Cook. James Palmer was licensed to preach in 1791.

Revolutionary war and was counted among the active patriots. He was not a scholar, but was a good student and an acceptable preacher. He was sometimes laid aside by ill health, but continued to minister till his death in 1810. At the ordination of Mr. Wood, Rev. James Manning, D.D., President of Brown University, preached the sermon.

In 1816, this church was greatly revived and enlarged, as were the other churches about this time. Rev. Mr. Peck, who was their minister two years, seems to have been the successful agent in the prosperity of the church, though in his memorandum of it he manifests his great modesty in referring only very slightly to himself.

Rev. John Mason Peck was born in Litchfield, South Farms, and was trained in the school of industry and frugality. He came to Amenia when a young man, and although his education was limited, he engaged in teaching awhile and then became a minister of the church. In 1816, he went to Philadelphia to complete his education, and thence to Missouri, where he spent the remainder of his life in preaching and in the cause of higher education. A pleasing memorial of this excellent man has been prepared by Rev. Rufus Babcock, D.D.

THE METHODISTS

The Methodist Society of Amenia, which was one of the earliest in this part of the country, seems to have been formed in 1788, and numbered eight members,[43] David Rundall being the only male member for several years. The first sermon was preached in a private house, half a mile east of Sharon Station, and the first hymn sung begins "Thou Judge of Quick and Dead." The meetings were held in that house, or in the neighborhood, till the settlers from Rhode Island removed here – Wardwell, the Ingrahams and others – when a society was formed near the Old Red Meeting House. It is understood that Mr. Garrettson formed the first class but he did not preach the first sermon. Captain Allen Wardwell was the first class leader.

The late Rev. Dr. Wakely called that part of Amenia "The Old Methodist Classic Ground." The important position of this society at that time may be inferred from the fact that the New York Annual Conference was held here. It was in 1808, and the sessions were held in the Round Top School House, about a half a mile northeast of the Old Red Meeting House. Rev. Bishop Asbury presided and occupied the teacher's chair,[44] with the school desk before him, and the preachers sat upon the benches of the pupils. On the Sabbath, the Conference oc-

---

43   These were David Rundall, his wife Catherine, his wife's mother, Ruth Powers, wife of Peter, Ruth Powers, wife of Frederick, and three others.

44   This chair is preserved as a commemorative relic.

cupied the Red Meeting House, when the Bishop preached.

One hundred and three preachers were stationed at the Conference. Ten were admitted on trial, one of whom was William Jewett. Fifteen were continued on trial; one of these was Phineas Rice. Eight were ordained elders, and one of the eight was Samuel Cochran.

Some families entertained ten or twelve of the preachers, and their horses, and the people were so gratified with the Conference that a committee waited on them with thanks for holding the session there, and invited them to come again.

The first church edifice of this society was built in 1812, a short distance east of the residence then of Thomas Ingraham, which remained until 1845. The New York Conference met in this church in 1813, when Bishops Asbury and McKendree presided.

At this Conference eighty-six preachers were stationed – the Conference having been divided since 1808. At this session of the Conference, David Rundall entertained fourteen of the preachers.

George and Thomas Ingraham and Frederick Powers were pillars in this church for many years, and Peter Powers was widely known as an able exhorter and venerated leader. The first preachers who went out from this vicinity were Robert and Elijah Hebard; many others have followed and the influence of the membership has gone into all parts of the land. The Amenia Seminary, which has accomplished so much for the cause of good education, was the result of their enterprise.

THE CHURCH AT THE CITY

Of the church at the City,[45] in the west part of the town, there are no very early records. The oldest record now known begins, "The Records of the church of Christ in the towns of Amenia, Washington, and Stanford, Dutchess county, A.D. 1787, commonly known by the name of the United Congregational Church of Westfield Society." Then again, April 9, 1787, a solemn fast was held and two sermons were delivered, one by the Rev. John Cornwall, the other by the Rev. Blackleach Burritt, after which the following persons signed the covenant."[46]

During the year 1787 thirty-six other names were added.

This could not have been the first institution of religious worship and of the ordinances by that people, as there was a house of worship

---

45 The "City" received that name, at the first settlement of the place, because three log houses were built near each other.

46 Those who first signed the covenant of 1787 were Stephen Kinney, Robert Willson, Timothy Wheeler, Joshua Wells, Jun., John Curtis, Selah Wells, Wm. Bell, Elizabeth Willson, Elizabeth Wheeler, Mary Curtis, Rebecca Shumday, Abigail Kinney, Anna Elliott, Anna Adams. Afterwards, Asa Hollister, Elisha Adams, Roger Southerland, Thomas Willson, Henry Kinney, Isaac Hunting, Robert Willson, Jun., Joel Smith, John Slawter, Elijah Allen, Benj. Denton, &c.

erected there in 1750, which gave place to another in 1814, both on the site of the present church edifice.[47] That so many were ready to enter into covenant that year, and that they had a name by which they were "commonly known," indicate that this was a re-organization, or a more perfect organization of a Christian community.

In 1812, July 7, "The Society unanimously voted that the church would give the Rev. Eli Hyde[48] a call to preach at the City Meeting-house, Smithfield Society, with this proviso, that all proper means be used to unite the two societies, and that the meetings be proportioned at the two houses as they shall agree."

The other "Society" and "House" refer to the Separate Meeting-house and Society,[49] which was located about two miles south of the City.

There are no records whatever or traditions that shows the origin of that society, or of its name, or of the reason of any division among this excellent Christian people. Perhaps the cause of any strife is now happily forgotten.

It is a reasonable theory, suggested by the name, and by a history[50] of the times, that a part of the church at the City became Separatists, or New Lights, and withdrew from the old church, in the early history of the congregation, when so many of the churches were agitated by that schism. The conservative and safer sentiments[51] of the congregation seems to have prevailed pretty soon, and harmony was evidently restored, as we find the leading men of both parties associated in the interests of the congregations many years previous to the final organic union.

---

47 In front of this church edifice was a little grove of oaks – one of which remains. Under the shade of this grove a great congregation were assembled, June 20, 1770, and heard a sermon by that wonderful preacher, George Whitefield. Every place where he ministered seems to have been remembered, and all who heard his discourse rehearsed it to the generations that came after them.

48 Rev. Eli Hyde came to this church from Oxford, Chenango county, N.Y. Rev. Job Swift, D.D., afterwards of Bennington, Vt., was minister at the City in 1782.

49 The Separate Meeting-house – now standing – was built some years before the Revolutionary war. Rev. John Cornwall, of Cornwall, Conn., resided near and ministered there many years.

50 See Contemporary history.

51 There were in the City a number of families from Long Island, and other places in New York, who had enjoyed a high degree of culture and religious instruction, who were evidently on the moderate side of those agitations.

THE OBLONG SOCIETY

The congregation in the Oblong valley was made up partly by families living in Connecticut, and the house of worship was at Amenia Union, and situated about twenty yards west of the colony line, on the hill west of E. Lambert's store, on land now owned by Wm. Blithman. It was a capacious building, with pews and galleries, and with doors on three sides. The roof had four sides, which terminated at the top in an ornamental cupola, which gave it the name of the "Round Top Meeting House." It was built previous to 1755,[52] and in 1786 it was taken down and another erected near where the present church edifice of the Society is situated.

The first preaching there, of which there is any record, was by a Moravian missionary, as we have seen in 1753. He was a German, and was naturally attached to the families of his countrymen settled here.

The congregation was composed of people of very diverse origin, Palatines, Huguenots, and Puritans, and their pastor was from Scotland. But a common desire for the ordinances of the gospel soon united them into a well-organized society.

The church was organized Dec. 11, 1759,[53] and the Rev. Ebenezer Knibloe was installed pastor.

He was from Scotland, and received his education in Edinburgh, and came to this country in 1752. It was while he was a student of theology at Edinburgh that the leaders in Scotland made that last bold strike in behalf of Prince Edward the Pretender, and the battle of Preston Plains was fought, which decided the fate of the unhappy prince. Mr. Knibloe, with some other young men, went out to witness the battle, and thus excited suspicion of the government that he sympathized with the party of the Prince, which made it desirable for him to flee away.

Mr. Knibloe came to the Oblong from Philips Manor, in Putnam county, near "Mr. Kent's Parish."[54]

He was pastor of the church at Oblong about sixteen years, and the breach of this relation was brought about in consequence of his apparent loyalty to the British King at the beginning of the Revolutionary war – an attitude entirely contrary to that of the Presbyterian ministers of

---

52 Deacon Ebenezer Hamlin, who died in 1755, bequeathed "'twenty-four pounds, old tenor, towards the worship of God in the neighborhood where I dwell,' viz., in or near the new-erected meeting-house, on the Oblong, near Sharon." (Sedgwick's History)

53 In 1859 the congregation of South Amenia held a memorial service in commemoration of the one hundredth anniversary, and a historic discourse was read.

54 The son of Mr. Kent, and the father of Chancellor Kent, was a friend of Mr. Knibloe.

that day. But the evidence is clearly against the suspicion, through his conscientious regard to duty, from which he could not be driven, and perhaps some tenacity of will, led him to pray in public for the King and the Royal family, which was sufficient in that excited condition of the public mind to raise the charge of disloyalty to his adopted country. It afterward became the conviction of the people that Mr. Knibloe was not disloyal, and from about the end of the war till the close of his life in 1785, he continued to preach to the acceptance of the people.[55]

In answer to the charge of disloyalty, Mr. Knibloe says, "When I read the ministerial charge, it was to go forth and preach the gospel of Jesus Christ. I look on it that government has nothing to do in the province of religion but to guard the empire of truth from every persecution, and leave the kingdom of heaven to its own Lord." "I am conscious to myself that I have ever wished and prayed for the welfare, happiness, liberty, and charter privileges of the British colonies in North America; likewise for the deliverance of our distressed brethren in Boston, and also for success to attend the armament and military preparations, which have already gone forth and are about to march in defense of American liberty."

This appears to have been written about the time of the battle of Bunker Hill, when all eyes were turned towards Boston.

While the British army held New York, the distinguished Dr. John Rodgers, pastor of the Presbyterian church there, left the city, as many others did, and found a safe retreat in the country.[56] He came here in 1778, and ministered to the people about two years. He was regarded with the highest respect by the people, and his influence was in the highest degree salutary. His biographer says that "through the influences of his ministrations in Amenia the congregation was greatly benefitted and improved and the former harmony restored." The Rev. Dr. Livingston also spent time with the congregation during the war; also Rev. David Rose,[57] who was a pastor of a Presbyterian church on Long Island.

The names of about a hundred sixty heads of families are recorded, most of whom were parishioners[58] of Mr. Knibloe, which indicates a population[59] nearly equal to the present in the same limits. The number

---

55 The house, which Mr. Knibloe built for himself, is about half a mile southeast of Amenia Union. His sons were John, William, Elijah, and Joseph. The three first named died in the great epidemic of 1812. Mr. Stephen Knibloe is his grandson.
56 There was no more safe retreat than this, nor any place in the land more completely out of the way of the disturbing effects of the war.
57 Rev. David Rose was a graduate of Yale.
58 The first deacons in Mr. Knibloe's church were Samuel Waterman and Meltiah Lothrop. Thomas Delano was elected in 1772, and Moses Barlow in 1775.
59 The population of Amenia in 1790 was 3,078.

of baptisms was 581 – delightful testimonies to the prosperity eof the generation.

These are some of the members of Mr. Knibloe's church: — Alexander Spencer, Ellis Doty, Joseph Chamberlain, and his wife, Abigail, Meltiah Lothrop, Daniel Rowley, Silas Belding, and his wife, Samuel Waterman, and his wife, Isaac Hamlin, and his wife, Benjamin Hollister, and wife, Benjamin Hollister, Jun., and wife, Daniel Castle, and wife, Ezra Reed, and wife, James Reed, Elijah Reed, and wife, Reuben Swift, Stephen Warren, and wife, Colbe Chamberlain, and wife, Moses Barlow, and wife, Eliakim Reed, and wife, Margaret Chamberlain, Priscilla Lovel, Jediah Bumpas, Hannah Swift, Dorcas Belding, Joanna Barlow, and many others.

The leading members of the Society in 1786, when the removed and rebuilt the church edifice, and in 1796, when they purchased the Parsonage Farm,[60] were these, James Reed, Moses Barlow, Walter Lothrop, Stephen Warren, Gideon Castle, Eliakim Reed, Elisha Barlow, Seth Swift, Moses Swift, Benjamin Delamater, Conrad Row, Samuel Row, Nicholas Row, Oliver Kellogg, Elisha Tobey, Ebenezer Hatch, Reuben Allerton, John Cline, John Boyd, Amariah Winchester, Amariah Hitchcock, Sylvanus Nye, William Young, Samuel Hitchcock, Ezekiel Sackett, Martin Delamater, Gershom Reed, Jedidiah Bump, and Azariah Judson.

The condition of the congregation, so many years, affirms the testimony to the value of a pious, learned, and stable ministry.

After the close of the Revolution, there was evidently a decline of religion in this congregation, as in others of the town, and perhaps from the same causes, which seemed to be the distracting spirit of the times; and not till about 1812 was there the beginning of a return to prosperity in these churches.[61]

After the death of Mr. Knibloe, several ministers were employed temporarily, and for short periods, till 1802, when Rev. John Barnet, A.M., was engaged for an indefinite time, and his ministry was acceptably continued till 1812, the time of his service including 1802 and 1812.

Mr. Barnet was a native of Simsbury, Conn., and was a graduate of Yale College, where he was, after the war, a tutor. He was a thorough scholar, and a successful teacher of young men, many of whom he had

60 In 1796, the Society bought the farm of Eliphalet Everett — the west part of J. H. Cline's farm – 160 acres, for a parsonage, for which they paid 660 pounds — $1650.

61 There is in these societies, as in all other agricultural communities, a serious decrease of attendants upon public worship, owing to a general decrease of rural population, particularly of the native laboring people, whose place is filled by foreigners of opposite religious attachments.

under his instruction while in Amenia.[62]

In the revolutionary war, Mr. Barnet was a chaplain, first in Col. Hopkin's regiment of Amenia at Saratoga, and afterwards in the regular army, where he was highly regarded by Washington.

Mr. Barnet's preaching was didactic and logical, rather that practical; instructive to a certain class, but not effective with the many. It was unfortunate for the congregation that he did not consider himself their pastor, but only a hired preacher, and, consequently, he omitted those services of a pastor, which are essential to the highest success of the ministry.

A Fourth of July oration by Mr. Barnet in 1812 was published; also a funeral sermon for Ambrose Spencer, Jun., who was killed at the battle of Lundy's Lane. Capt. Spencer had been a pupil of Mr. Barnet in Amenia, and though very young, was aid to General Brown when mortally wounded July 25, 1814.

In 1815, the scattered remains of the old church were gathered together, and with considerable additions, a reorganization was effected. Rev. Joel Osborn became the pastor, and from that time there has been a regular succession of settled pastors to the present.

---

[62] Among the pupils of Mr. Barnet in Amenia were Abraham Bockee, Allen Hollister, Perlee, Fish, and several sons of Hon. Ambrose Spencer. Mrs. Barnet was a sister of Judge Spencer. Mr. Barnet died at the residence of his son in Greene county in 1837.

CIVIL ORGANIZATION

The "Precinct" of Amenia was formed by an act of the Colonial Legislature, March 20, 1762. The geographical limits were the same also of the "town" of Amenia, which was formed March 7, 1788, and continued the same till March 26, 1823, when the towns of Amenia and Northeast were so reorganized as to change the boundary between them as it is at present. This territory had been a part of Crum Elbow Precinct,[63] and was about twelve miles in length, and of an average width of four and a half miles.

The name Amenia was first used about the time of the organization of the Precinct, and owes its origin[64] to Dr. Thomas Young, a learned gentleman who resided several years at Amenia Union, where he married a daughter of Capt. Garret Winegar.

Hon. Egbert Benson, in a Memoir read before the N.Y. Historical Society,[65] in 1816, says "Vermont – green mountains – and the town of Amenia – pleasant – owe their names to the fancy of Young, the poet. I mean the American, and not the English Young. He had a peculiar facility in making English words from Latin ones."

Dr. Young was the author of a poem,[66] called "The Conquest of Quebec," in which he gives an account of the provincial troops that were sent from the several towns to aid in that campaign under Wolfe, which resulted in the capture of Quebec. He was a friend of Ethan Allen,[67] who resided in Salisbury,[68] Conn., while the former resided in Amenia, and they were often together, and they were also in sympathy

---

63 The municipal regulations of a precinct were nearly the same as a town. At the first Precinct meeting, "It was resolved that the thanks of this meeting be given to Robert Livingston and Henry Livingston, for their favor and regard to the Precinct of Amenia in procuring a division of the same." – that is a separation from the larger precinct. Crum Elbow Precinct extended from the Hudson River to the Connecticut line. Charlotte Precinct was west of Amenia. Crum, or Krom, seems to have been the name of a family in the west part of the Precinct. Crum Elbow ("Crom Ebogh") Creek enters the Hudson there.

64 The name is from a Latin word, which signifies pleasant. "Amoena. Pleasant. De locis praecipue dicitur." – applied principally to places. Though so suitable a name, and agreeable, it had not been given to any other town in the country.

65 P. 126, N.Y. Hist. Collection, Vol. ii.

66 Only a few lines of the poem are now known.

67 "Appendix to Early History of Vermont" says of Young, "He was highly distinguished as a philosopher, philanthropist and patriot, and for his erudition and brilliancy of imagination." Dr. Young is supposed to have died in Philadelphia in 1777, leaving in America two accomplished daughters.

68 Ethan Allen was one of the three men who built the first blast furnace in Salisbury.

in the violence of their patriotism and in their religious unbelief.

FIRST TOWN MEETING

The record of the first town meeting is this: — "At the Annual Town Meeting of the Freeholders and Inhabitants of the Precinct of Amenia, on the first Tuesday of April, Anno Domini 1762, at the house[69] of Roswell Hopkins, Esq., Michael Hopkins was chosen Clerk of said Precinct, and Capt. Stephen Hopkins was chosen Supervisor.

Samuel Doty and Jonathan Reynolds were chosen Assessors for the year ensuing.

Benjamin Benedict, Abraham Paine, and Moses Barlow were chosen Overseers of the Poor.

Conrad Winegar was chosen Collector and Constable.

Samuel Shepherd, Rufus Herrick, and Ichabod Rogers were chosen Constables.

Thomas Wolcott and Jonathan Reynolds were Pound Keepers.

Captain Stephen Hopkins and Samuel King were chosen to take Inventories of Intestate Estates for the year ensuing.

Miles Washburn, Benjamin Benedict, and Roswell Hopkins were chosen Fence Viewers for the year ensuing.

Thomas Wolcott, John Beebe, Joseph Pennoyer, Philip Pitts, Samuel Shepherd, William Barker, William Roberts, Edmund Perlee, Moses Harris, and Job Milk were chose Overseers of Highways.

Also voted that a Fence, four feet and four inches high, well-wrought and substantial, shall be deemed lawful."

In 1763, Edmund Perlee was chosen Supervisor.

In 1764, 1765, 1766, Stephen Hopkins was chosen Supervisor.

In 1767, Edmund Perlee was chosen.

In 1768 and 1769, Ephraim Paine was Supervisor.

In 1770, Abraham Bockee was chosen Moderator of the Town meeting and Ephraim Paine was chosen Supervisor, and continued to 1776.

In 1776, Silas Marsh was chosen Supervisor, and in 1777 and 1778, Roswell Hopkins.

In 1779 and 1780, Dr. John Chamberlain.

---

69   The place of the first Town Meeting, and of subsequent Town Meetings for many years, was near where the Old Meeting House stood. The house of Roswell Hopkins stood near the Meeting House. The residence of his father, Capt. Stephen Hopkins, who was the first Supervisor, was further south towards the fair grounds, and was in later years reached by a lane from the highway. Mr. Henry Ingraham resided there several years. The Totten house, where Mr. Perlee lived, was built by one of the sons of Capt. Stephen Hopkins. The Town meeting was held at Capt. Abiah Palmer's first in 1789. There was no highway east from Amenia. Where the turnpike now runs there was a swamp. There was a road running east and west across the hill north of Hiram Cooper's.

In 1781, Colbe Chamberlain.

In 1782 and 1783, Ephraim Paine.

In 1784, Isaac Darrow was Supervisor.

Michael Hopkins was Town Clerk till 1773, when Roswell Hopkins was chosen and continued till 1784.

Capt. Stephen Hopkins and Samuel King continued to take Inventories of Intestate Estate for several years.

The Justices of the Peace – from the Crown, of course – were Abraham Bocka, Ephraim Paine, Roswell Hopkins, and Conrad Winegar.

In 1772, Ezra Reed, Job Milk, and Elijah Wheeler were chosen Overseers of the Poor, "and are to serve for nothing."

CIVIL LIST

The following named citizens of Amenia have served in various official positions.

Ephraim Paine was Deputy to the First New York Provincial Congress in 1775.[70]

Jacob Evertson was a Deputy to the N.Y. CIAL Congress in 1776.

Ephraim Paine was a delegate in Congress[71] under the Articles of Confederation in 1784.

Ephraim Paine was a member of the N.Y. Senate from Middle District in 1779, 1780, 1784 and 1785.

Reuben Hopkins, a native of Amenia, was a member of N.Y. Senate from Middle District from 1794 to 1797.

Elisha Barlow was a member of N.Y. Senate from Middle District[72] from 1807 and 1810.

Abraham Bockee was a member of N.Y. Senate from 1842 to 1845.

Abiah W. Palmer was a member of N.Y. Senate 1868-69 and 1872-73.

Edmund Perlee was a member of the Constitutional Convention of 1801.

Elisha Barlow was a member of the Constitutional Convention of 1821.

---

70 This Provincial Congress convened in New York, May 23, 1775, and adjourned November 4, 1775. Col. Anthony Hoffman, Gilbert Livingston, and Richard Montgomery were among the delegates from Dutchess county.

71 The number of delegates in that Congress from this State were seven. Of these were Egbert Benson, John Jay, &c.

72 The Middle District was composed of Dutchess, Orange, and Ulster counties.

MEMBERS OF ASSEMBLY
OF STATE OF NEW YORK FROM AMENIA

Brinton Paine, 1775-81 and 1785-87.
Abraham Paine, 1781-82.
Barnabas Paine, 1793.
James Bockee, 1794.
Jacob Bockee, 1795-97.
Wm. Barker, 1798, 1800.
Platt Smith, 1798-99.
Elisha Barlow, 1800, 1802.
Benajah Thompson, 1804, 1808, 1809.
Benjamin Herrick, 1806.
Cyrenus Crosby, 1808.
Alexander Neely, 1810-11.
Joel Benton, 1814, '15, '17, and '31.
Isaac Smith, 1816.
Abraham Bockee, 1820.
Taber Belden, 1828, '37.
Joel Brown, 1833.
Henry Conklin, 1833, '34, '39, and '40.
John K. Mead, 1844.
Amos Bryant, 1840.
Walter Sherman, 1845, '47.
James Hammond, 1848-49.
Wm. H. Bostwick, 1854.
Abiah Palmer, 1860.

OTHER OFFICES HELD BY CITIZENS OF AMENIA

Ephraim Paine was appointed First Judge of Dutchess county in 1778, which was also the first appointment to the office of Judge in Dutchess county after the organization of the government of the State of New York.

Abraham Bockee was appointed First Judge of Dutchess county in 1846.

Elisha Barlow was one of the Judges of the County Court in 1808.

Abraham Bockee was member of the U.S. Congress in 1829-31 and 1833-37.

Ebenezer Nye was Surrogate of Dutchess county in 1821.

John Brush was Surrogate in 1819.

E.M. Swift was District Attorney in 1843, and B. Platt Carpenter in 1858.

Thomas N. Perry was Sheriff in 1840, and Judah Swift in 1861.

Jacob B. Carpenter was Presidential Elector in 1861.

Hon. William H. Leonard, son of Dr. Leonard, and native of Amenia, was elected one of the Judges of Supreme Court in 1859, and was afterwards one of the Judges of the court of Appeals, and was also Commissioner of the Court of Appeals.

Hon. George G. Reynolds, of Amenia, is now, 1875, serving as one of the Judges of the City Court of Brooklyn.

Hon. William I. Cornwall, of Cayuga county, son of Eden Cornwall, and grandson of Rev. John Cornwall, has been several times Member of the Assembly and of the Senate.

THE REVOLUTIONARY WAR

In the war of the Revolution the patriotism of the citizens of Amenia was expressed with promptness and almost entire unanimity. On the 29th of April 1775, only ten days after the battle of Lexington, a meeting was held in the city of New York of those ready to oppose the oppressive acts of the British government. An Association was formed and a Pledge adopted, which was sent for signatures into every county of the State.

THE PLEDGE

"Persuaded that the salvation of the rights and liberties of America depend, under God, on the firm union of his inhabitants in a vigorous prosecution of the measures necessary for its safety, and convinced of the necessity of preventing anarchy and confusion which attend a dissolution of the powers of government, We, the Freemen, Freeholders, and Inhabitants of Amenia, being greatly alarmed at the avowed design of the Ministry to raise a revenue in America, and shocked by the bloody scene now acting in Massachusetts Bay, do in the most solemn manner resolve never to become slaves, and do associate, under all the ties of religion, honor, and love to our country, to adopt and endeavor to carry into execution whatsoever measures may be recommended by the Continental Congress, or resolved upon by our Provincial Convention, for the purpose of preserving our constitution and of opposing the several arbitrary acts of the British Parliament, until a reconciliation between Great Britain and America, on constitutional principles (which we most ardently desire) can be obtained; and that we will in all things follow the advice of our General Committee respecting the purposes aforesaid, the preservation of peace and good order and the safety of individuals and property."

This Pledge of the "Association" was presented to the citizens of Amenia for their signatures in June and July of 1775, by Roswell Hopkins, Samuel King, and Silas Marsh, a committee appointed for that purpose, and four hundred and twenty subscribed to the pledge, and only six delayed or refused to sign.

Those who persisted in refusing to sign were Joel Harvey, Philip Row, Samuel Dunham, Judah Swift, and Peter Slason.[73]

---

73   Mr. Slason never accepted the situation. He lived in South Amenia near his brother-in-law, Capt. Wm. Chamberlain, and after the war, when the pole was raised in that part of town, crowned with the cap of liberty, Mr. Slason was brought to it with a rope around his neck and required to confess his loyalty. He kneeled down before this emblem of the nation's freedom and cried out, "Great art thou, O Baal."

The qualifications in their subscription to the pledge by three of the justices of the peace of the town, shows a scrupulous conscientiousness rather than any want of patriotism; and their regard for their oath of office rather gives a serious emphasis to their act. Isaac Smith subscribed with this limitation, "I do agree to the above Association so far that it does not interfere with the oath of my office, nor my allegiance to the King. - Isaac Smith." Abraham Bockee made this qualification "Not to infringe on my oaths. - Abraham Bockee."

John Garnsey refused at first, and afterwards gave this declaration. - "June 8, 1775. This may certify to all people whom it may concern that I, the subscriber, am willing to do what is just and right to secure the privileges of America, both civil and sacred, and to follow the advice of our reverend Congress, so far as they do the Word of God and the example of Jesus Christ, and I hope, in the grace of God, no more will be required. As witness my hand. John Garnsey."

This stern old Puritan distinctly asserted the principles of the "higher law," and he was not less heroic in asserting the rights of men.

Those who signed the Pledge of Association were called "Associators," [74] and the subscription to the Pledge was pressed upon individuals - with a degree of rigor, perhaps, sometimes - as a test of their loyalty.[75]

A Committee of Safety was appointed here as in other towns in the country. Besides those already mentioned, Capt. Wm. Chamberlain, in the east part of town, was very active. The vigilance of the Committee was particularly directed to the movements of the Tories, or those suspected of a want of loyalty to the country, and any hesitation in signing the pledge was the occasion of suspicion and accusation awhile, to the disturbance of society, and the violent zeal of some of the leaders led them to rebuke the moderation of others who were equally steadfast in their patriotism. It is quite probable that some may have been brought to a decision by the prompt and vigorous measures of the Committee. It became evident, however, that a most remarkable unanimity of loyal sentiment prevailed in the town, while in many other towns of the county a very large number were openly hostile to the action of the patriots.

A rude prison, constructed of logs, was used for confining tories and any other suspected persons. This was built about a half mile east of the present village of Amenia[76] and north of where the turnpike now runs. The remains of this prison were there a few years ago.

74　The list was sometimes called the "Roll of Honor."

75　Mr. Marsh, in his return of names to the committee, says, "I am compelled to remind you of James Smith - out of my limits - who is notoriously wicked."

76　The reader will bear in mind that there was no village where Amenia now is, no highway where the turnpike now runs, and that the central place of public business of the town was by the Red Meeting House, by the burying ground.

THE CENTENNIAL

The returning Centennial of each important act in the great drama of the Revolution is now celebrated with appropriate ceremonies, that there may be kept alive in the minds of all the people a just estimate of the work of their fathers, and of the principles which were asserted at such a cost. It is now just a hundred years since the citizens of Amenia by this subscription put their hand to the work of the Revolution; and we are, at this distance of time, better able to estimate the character of that important act.

It is certain that a very large proportion of those that joined in the pledge were all well informed on the questions at issue and knew the serious nature of their action. This is intimated by the religious regard they had for their oaths. The civil and religious rights of individuals and the limits of state authority had been subjects of their study all their lives.[77] Persecution had driven some of them from homes in the old country, and others, who came out of New England, had been educated to a very jealous sense of personal responsibility and personal rights. They were not led in haste by any political faction to rash excitement. They understood the central truth of the Revolution, — that is was not a rebellion, but a positive assertion of rights which they had always justly held, and a determined resistance to newly imposed bonds.

It is not any less to the honor of their patriotic virtue and courage that they did not foresee the greatness of the end of this incipient act; that, with the great leaders of the people, in the beginning of the contest, "They builded wiser than they knew."

---

77 It is recommended by the General Assembly of the Presbyterian Church that a memorial discourse be preached in every Presbyterian church on the Sabbath, preceding the 4th of July, 1876, to preserve the history of that church, and to commemorate the patriotism of the ministers and Christian people of the Revolution. A large number of these members of the patriotic league were members of the Christian societies of the town.

ROLL OF HONOR
Names of the Citizens of Amenia who subscribed the Pledge

The names if those patriotic citizens, who did not hesitate to show their hands in this serious crisis, are fortunately preserved and are recorded now, as a fit memorial of their loyalty and courage, which will be regarded with just pride by those who recognize in these names those of their ancestors and relatives, and former citizens of Amenia.

More than three hundred of these names are mentioned in other records of the town, or are known as belonging to families then residents. One hundred and fifty of these, or more, were independent, separate landholders.

Several of the patriots must have been absent. Ephraim Paine was attending the Provincial Congress. Benjamin and Waight Hopkins had already gone with Ethan Allen. Reuben Hopkins, Jacob Bockee, and some others, who are known to have been true, are not mentioned.

The number of names given with those added which are known, making 435, gives some intimation of the population of the town at that time.

The present spelling of the names of families is adopted, as the manuscript in many cases seems to have been very uncertain.

Thomas Ackley
Abraham Adams
Abraham Adams, Jun.
Elisha Adams
Jonas Adams
Joseph Adams
William Adams
James Allen
Jonathan Allerton
James Allsworth, Jun.
William Allsworth
Solomon Armstrong
Cornelius Atherton
Benjamin Atwater
John Atwater
Levi Atwater
Joseph Backus
James Barker
William Barker
Elisha Barlow
Moses Barlow
Nathan Barlow
Henry Barnes
Josiah Barnes
James Barnet
John Barnet
John Barnet, Jun.
Daniel Barry
John Barry
John Barton
James Beadle
Elisha Beardsley
John Benedict

Samuel Benedict
John Benson
Joseph Benson
Ebenezer Besse
Elias Besse
Ephraim Besse
James Betts
Daniel Balkely
William Blunt
Abraham Bockee
John Boyd
Jared Brace
Edmund Bramhall
David Brewster
Ellis Briggs
Benjamin Brown
David Brown
Moses Brown
Zedekiah Brown
John Brunson, Jun.
John Bronson
Lemuel Brush
Richard Brush
William Brush
Ezra Bryan
Israel Buck
Jonathan Buck
Zadock Buck
Grover Buel
Grover Buel, Jun.
Jedidiah Bump
Eli Burton
Isaac Burton

Isaac Burton, Jun.
Judah Burton
Ebenezer Carter
Daniel Carter
Gideon Castle
Colbe Chamberlain
John Chamberlain
William Chamberlain
Increase Child
James Chapman
Ezra Cleaveland
Josiah Cleaveland
John Cline
Peter Cline
Led. Ch. (?)
John Coe
Barnabas Cole
David Collin
John Collin
John Connor
Joab Cook
Simeon Cook
Simeon Cook, Jun.
Nathaniel Cook
Samuel Cornwall
Thomas Cornwall
William Cornwall
Jabez Crippen
Benjamin Crippen
Benjamin Crofut
Enoch Crosby
John Curry
Elijah Darley
Mathew Dagget, Jun.
Caleb Dakin
Isaac Darrow
Daniel Davidson
Squire Davis
Isaac Delamater
John Delamater
Martin Delamater
Benjamin Delano
Stephen Delano
Joseph Delavergne
Lewis Delavergne

John Denny, Jun.
Abraham Denton
Benjamin Denton
Benjamin Denton, Jun.
Joel Denton
John Denton
Gabriel Dickinson
Versal Dickinson
James Dickson
Samuel Dodge
John Dunham
Nehemiah Dunham
Samuel Dunham, Jr.
Seth Dunham
Benjamin Doty
David Doty
Joseph Doty
Reuben Doty
Jacob Dorman
John Douglass
John Drake
Jacob Elliot
Archibald Farr
John Farr
Albert Finch
William Finch
Jonathan Fish
Asa Fort
Ephraim Ford
James Ford
John Ford
William Ford
Nathaniel Foster
Benjamin Fowler
Joseph Fowler
Elijah Freeman
John Freeman
Robert Freeman
Robert Freeman, Jun.
Abraham French
John Furman
Thomas Ganong
Daniel Garnsey
John Garnsey
Gerard Gates

John Gates
Nathaniel Gates
Nathaniel Gates, Jun.
Stephen Gates
Abner Gillett
Barnabas Gillett
David Gillett
Gardner Gillett
Joseph Gillett
Moses Gillett
Eleazar Gillson
Jeduthan Gray
Joseph Gray
Samuel Gray
Joseph Green
Timothy Green
William Hall
Richard Hamilton
Jason Hammond
Sylvester Handly
Daniel Harvey
Obed Harvey
Obed Harvey, Jun.
Moses Harris, Jun.
Samuel Hart
Abel Hebard
James Hebard
Robert Hebard
Benjamin Herrick
Benjamin Herrick, Jun.
Nathan Herrick
Rufus Herrick
Samuel Herrick
Stephen Herrick
Stephen Herrick, Jun.
William Herrick
Abner Holmes
Benjamin Holmes
Elijah Holmes
Ichabod Holmes
John Holmes
Samuel Holmes
Benjamin Hollister
Samuel Hollister
Noah Hopkins

Roswell Hopkins
Asa Hudson
William Hunt
Jonathan Hunter
John Howard
Samuel Jarvis
Benjamin Johns
Eben Johnson
Ezekiel Johnson
Paul Johnson
Robert Johnson
Samuel Johnson
John Jones
Samuel Judson
Heath Kelly
Simeon Kelsey
Joel Ketchum
Samuel King
Samuel King, Jun.
William King
Ebenezer Kinney
Elijah Kinney
Jesse Kinney
Stephen Kinney
William Knapp
Zadock Knapp
Daniel Lamb
David Lamb
Isaac Lamb
Thiel Lamb
Ebenezer Larabe
Richard Larabe
Joshua Lasell
Ebenezer Latimer
Elisha Latimer
Thomas Lawrence
Theophilus Lockwood
Walter Lothrop
John Lloyd
Isaac Marks
Isaiah Marsh
Silas Marsh
William McCullough
John McNeil
Levi Mahew

Thaddeus Manning
Obed Matthews
Benjamin Maxam
Daniel May
Ebenezer Mayo
Elijah Mayo
Isaiah Mead
James Mead
Job Mead
John Mead
King Mead
John Mears
Abel Merchant
John Merchant
Job Milk
Wright Millman
William Mitchell
John Mordack
Thomas Morey
Peter Morse
Eleazer Morton
Abial Mott
William Moulton
Thomas Mygatt
Sylvanus Nye
Levi Orton
Isaac Osborn
John Osborn
Josiah Osborn
Owen Osterhout
Abraham Paine
Barnabas Paine
Barnabas Paine, Jun.
Brinton Paine
David Paine
Elihu Paine
Ichabod Paine
Ichabod Paine, Jun.
James Paine
James Palmer
Nathan Palmer
Samuel Palmer
Ebenezer Park
Isaac Park
Robert Patrick

Amos Pennoyer
Joseph Pennoyer
Edmund Perlee
Jonathan Pike
Nathaniel Pinney
Elijah Porter
Jacob Powers
Joest Powers
Peter Probasco
Thorn Pudney
Monmouth Purdy
David Randle
Eliakim Reed
Elijah Reed
Ezra Reed
Gershom Reed
James Reed
Silas Reed
Simeon Reed
Jacob Reynolds
Stephen Reynolds
William Reynolds
William Roberts
Ichabod Rodgers
Ichabob Rodgers, Jun.
Silas Roe
Elijah Roe
Garret Row
James Row
Nicholas Row
Bezaleel Rudd
Zebulon Rudd
David Rundall
Jared Rundall
Ezekiel Sackett
John Sackett
John Sackett, Jun.
Richard Sackett
Benjamin Sage
Daniel Sage
Ezra St. John
John Scott
Rufus Seaton
John Seymour
Daniel Shepard

Israel Shepard
Jonathan Shepard
Samuel Shepard
Asahel Sherwood
Parrock Sherwood
Abner Shevalier
Elias Shevalier
Peter Shevalier
Richard Shevalier
Solomon Shevalier
Lemuel Shurtliff
Bowers Slason
Abraham Slocum
Elijah Smith
Elijah Smith, Jun.
Isaac Smith
James Smith, Jun.
Jesse Smith
Joseph Smith
Platt Smith
Thomas Smith
Samuel Snyder
George Sornborger
Frederick Sornborger
Samuel Southworth
Elnathan Spaulding
Jacob Spicer
Nathan Spicer
Andrew Stevens
Elkanah Stevens
Matthew Stevens
Lot Swift

Nathaniel Swift
Samuel Swift
Seth Swift
Joshua Talent
John Thayer
Beriah Thomas
Thomas Thomas
Samuel Thompson
Samuel Thompson, Jun.
Ezra Thornton
Joel Thurston
John Thurston
Timothy Tillson
John Torner
Seeley Trowbridge
David Truesdel
Adin Tubs
Shubal Tyler
Matthew Van Deusen
Benjamin Vaun
Stephen Warren
Daniel Washburn
Joel Washburn
David Waters
Samuel Waters
Daniel Webster
Thomas Welch
Josiah Wells
Samuel West
Noah Wheeler
Seth Wheeler
SolomonWheeler

NEWS OF THE BATTLE OF LEXINGTON

When the news of the battle of Lexington reached Amenia, the militia companies came together with a spontaneous will, like men who had something to do. "They were addressed by Ephraim Paine, Esq., in a masterly oration," in which he rehearsed the matters which had brought the country to so serious a crisis, pointed to the tyrannical measures of England, intended to enslave this country, now already begun in blood, the danger of America, and that the time had come to step forth with manly courage to resist the force of lawless invasion.

"At the close of this address," says one[78] who was present, "the whole audience, officers and privates, caught the flame as from an electric shock, and were ready to march to the seat of war." Simeon Cook, captain of one of the companies, addressed his men, "Fellow soldiers, the time is come to give up our liberties, or defend them with the musket. As many of you as are willing to march with me to the scene of action, I will lead, and I will expose myself to all the dangers and hardships that you will be exposed to. If any of you are unwilling to go you are dismissed." It is added that not one left the ranks.

---

78 Barnabas Paine, Esq., who left in writing many valuable statements of the times. He was the father of the late Barnabas Paine, Esq.

SOLDIERS IN THE REVOLUTIONARY WAR

These are names of the soldiers, as far as now ascertained, who were residents of Amenia:

Dr. Reuben Allerton
Barzilla Andrews
William Barker
Elisha Barlow
Daniel C. Bartlett
John Benedict
Samuel Benedict
William Blunt
Jacob Bockee
Jesse Brush
William Brush
James Bump
Judah Burton
Colbe Chamberlain
Conrad Chamberlain
William Chamberlain
Increase Child
Peter Cline
John Congdon
Nathan Conklin
Simeon Cook
Isaac Delamater
Joel Denton
David Doty
Reuben Doty
Stephen Edget
Jabez Flint
John Ford
Jeduthan Gray
Samuel Gray
Moses Harris
Lemuel Hatch
Oliver Hatch
Oliver Hatch

Asa Hollister
Ichabod Holmes
Benjamin Hopkins
Noah Hopkins
Reuben Hopkins
Roswell Hopkins
Waight Hopkins
Warum Kingsley
Jones Knapp
Ephraim Lord
Mackey
Job Mead
Job Mead, Jun.
Joseph Mitchell
Joshua Newman
Isaac Osborn
Brinton Paine
Amos Pennoyer
Jesse Pennoyer
Edmund Perlee
Jacob Powers
Silas Ray
James Reed
Samuel Reed
Silas Reed
Simeon Reed
Bezaleel Rudd
David Rundall
Roger Southerland
Alex. Spencer, Jun.
Samuel Waters
Noah Wheeler
Garret Winegar

OFFICERS IN THE WAR

The following notices of officers, who were residents of Amenia, are compiled from the Calendar of Historical Manuscripts, relating to the War of the Revolution.

July 27, 1775, Waight Hopkins was chosen Captain in a regiment of Green Mountain Boys under Colonel Ethan Allen and Lieut.-Col. Seth Warner.

Oct. 17, 1775, — The date of commissions to officers in Regiment No. 6, of Militia of Dutchess county.

David Southerland, Colonel
Roswell Hopkins, Lieutenant Colonel
Simeon Cook, Major
Richard DeCantalon, Major
Joseph Carpenter, Adjutant
Daniel Sheperd, Quarter-Master

First Company
William Barker, Capt.
Job Mead. 1st Lieut.
Noah Hopkins, 2d Lieut.
Abner Gillett, Ensign

Second Company
Brinton Paine, Capt.
Samuel Waters, 1st Lieut.
Ichabod Holmes, 2d Lieut.
Jesse Brush, Ensign

Third Company
Joshua Laselle, Capt.
Colbe Chamberlain, 1st Lieut.
David Doty, 2d Lieut.
Elisha Barlow, Ensign

Fourth Company
Robert Freeman, Capt.
Elijah Smith, 1st Lieut.
Ezra St. John, 2d Lieut.
Noah Wheeler, Ensign

Major DeCantelon was not a resident of Amenia, but was probably a professional soldier, appointed to that regiment for the instruction of the officers and men in military art.

Oct. 17, 1775, — Minutemen of Amenia Precinct. Regiment under Col. John Van Ness.

James Reed, Major
Reuben Hopkins, Adj.
Jos. Ketcham, Jr., Q. M.
Josiah Morse, Ensign

Increase Child, Capt.
John Lloyd, 1st Lieut.
William Blunt, 2d Lieut.

1775. – Officers in Gen. Clinton's Brigade recommended to him for standing army. –
Col. Graham
Capt. Brinton Paine
Lieut. Hopkins

1775. – Rufus Herrick was appointed Captain in a Dutchess county regiment.

April 12, 1776. – Officers in Col. James Clinton's regiment of Continentals, Increase Child, Capt. John Loyd, Lieut.

1776. – Petition of Officers of Col. Graham's regiment for the appointment of Dr. Abraham Teller to be Surgeon of said regiment.

Morris Graham, Col.	Roswell Hopkins, Lieut.-Col.
Wm. Barker, Major	Reuben Hopkins, Adj.
Elisha Barlow, Capt.	Stephen Edget, Lieut.
Samuel Waters, Lieut., and others.	

Oct. 1776. – Capt. Edget resigns on account of sickness.

Dec. 14, 1776. – In Committee of Arrangements, Resolved, the Brinton Paine, Esq., be appointed Capt. In Col. Dubois' regiment.

Nov. 15, 1776.— MOUNT INDEPENDENCE – Lieutenant David Doty has obtained leave of Major-Gen. Gates to join the N.Y. troops; we recommend the said Doty as a worthy officer and one that has performed his duty to universal satisfaction as Adjutant and Lieutenant.

NATHANIEL BUEL, Col.   JOHN SEDGWICK, Maj.

Jan. 1777. – Officers recommended for commissions according to their rank in Col. Humphrey's regiment.

Brinton Paine, Major	Edmund Perlee, 1st Lieut.
Wm. Chamberlain, Capt.	Reuben Doty, 2d Lieut.
John McNeil, 1st Lieut.	David Doty, Adj.

Jan. 7, 1777. – Capt. James Reed petitions to be relieved from the operation of the rules adopted in regard to the transportation of flour to the army at the eastward. Capt. Reed was Assistant Commissary, and was directed to send flour for the army at the east, but was hindered by a certain embargo on flour crossing the colony line. Judah Swift disregarded these orders of the Provincial authorities, and sent, in the night, two sleigh loads of flour to the east by way of Kent. On the Kent road, near the colony line, the drivers encountered a guard, whom they overpowered. The object of this embargo seems to have been to prevent the flour from going into the hands of the enemy. Trusty persons received a permit to go with the flour to certain points, and in several cases these persons agreed to bring back a load of salt.

Feb. 7-15, 1776. – Account of guns delivered to Capt. Child and appraised by Dr. Chamberlain, C. Marsh and C. Atherton.

		£	s	d
1 Gun of	Stephen Warren	3	0	0
1 " "	Levi Orton	1	10	0
1 " "	Jedidiah Bump	2	15	0
1 " "	Benjamin Delano.. ..	2	0	0
1 " "	Peter Cline	1	15	0
1 " "	Nathan Barlow	2	5	0
1 " "	Benjamin Hall	2	0	0
1 " "	Sylvanus Nye	3	15	0
1 " "	Gershom Reed	2	10	0
1 " "	Eliakim Reed	3	10	0
1 Pistol of	Joseph Pennoyer	0	10	0

This is taken from a memorandum found among the papers of Capt. James Reed. It shows the means to which Congress was obliged to resort to furnish firearms to the soldiers.

April 22, 1777. – Major Brinton Paine is a prisoner in New York, "and is not like to come out." "The Major tells the guards that he is in a just cause, and if he gets out he will fight them again."

April 1777. – The lead mines at Great Nine Partners were explored, with some success, by an agent of Congress. The lead mines were on the lands of Mr. Fish, in Amenia, and were explored at the suggestion of Moses Harris. The Commissioners appointed by the Provincial Congress were Jonathan Landon and Ezra Thompson, and they employed John McDonald, an experienced miner from Scotland, who appears to have come over for the purpose of aiding the people in their struggle. The work at these mines was continued through the season, as reported by Mr. McDonald with great particularity.

This John McDonald was of a distinguished Highland family of McDonalds, and his wife was the granddaughter of Rob Roy MacGregor, one of Walter Scott's heroes. Mr. McDonald was the father of John McDonald, well known in Dutchess county fifty years ago, and of Miss Anne McDonald, very extensively known on account of her position in Judge Smith's family. She came with her father from Scotland when a child, and on account of the reduction of his estate by the worthlessness of continental money, she entered Judge Smith's family as a governess. After Judge Smith's death, she became, through her remarkable executive ability, almost the sole manager of his very large estate, and continued in that position many years.[79]

Sept. 17, 1776. – Cornelius Atherton petitions the N.Y. Council for the exemption from military duty of his workman, engaged in the manufacture of fire-arms in his contract with Congress.[80]

NOTICES OF INDIVIDUAL SOLDIERS

"Captain Cook," says Mr. Paine, "was afterwards deservedly promoted to the rank of Major, and was distinguished for his courage and steadiness[81] in battle near Fort Independence,[82] in 1777." "It was in this action also that Captain Noah Wheeler and Col. Roswell Hopkins were noted for their bravery, and also privates Amos Pennoyer and Jeduthan Gray, who were all from Amenia."

Five sons[83] of Capt. Stephen Hopkins were officers, Waight and Benjamin joined the Green Mountain Boys under Col. Ethan Allen and Lieut.- Col. Seth Warner, and were both killed by the Indians. Roswell Hopkins was Colonel, and took part with his regiment in the battles at Saratoga. Dr. Reuben Allerton was Surgeon of the regiment in that campaign, and it is understood that Rev. John Barnet was Chaplain, who was afterwards Chaplain in the Continental army. Reuben Hopkins, the youngest of the brothers, and who was born in Amenia in 1748, was adjutant in Col. Graham's regiment. In the beginning of the war of 1812, he was appointed one of eight Brigadier Generals[84] of N.Y. State, being then a resident of Orange county.

Captain William Chamberlain was very active among the citizens of the town, as one of the Committee of Safety in the beginning of the war; and in 1777 he received a commission as Captain in Col. Humphrey's regiment, and entered the army under Gates, and took part in the battles at Saratoga, which resulted in the capture of Burgoyne.

Brinton Paine was transferred to the regular army in Col. Dubois'

---

79 The McDonald burying ground is in the northwest corner of old Amenia, near the Row Schoolhouse, where the several generations of the family in this country are buried.
80 He was engaged at the Steel Works.
81 Mr. Paine says that "Major Cook was a tall, spare man, and of singular steadiness of manner, which gave him the name among his neighbors of 'Old Steady.'"
82 This was the Fort Independence near Peekskill.
83 One had died.
84 Lossing's "War of 1812," page 366.

regiment, which was in Gen. Clinton's brigade. Col. Dubois had served in Canada, and he commanded the right wing at the battle of Klock's Field, near Mohawk, in 1780. In April 1777, Maj. Paine was a prisoner.

In Oct. 1777, the Militia of Dutchess county were called to the defense of the Highlands.[85]

Jacob Bockee was a Captain of a company in the regiment under the command of the gallant Col. Marinus Willett.

Moses Harris, Jun., served in the dangerous duty of a spy, and was greatly confided in by Washington. He was rewarded for his services, after the war, by a grant of land in Westfield, Washington county, N.Y., now the town of Fort Ann. Mr. Harris resided in the northwest part of town.

"Alexander Spencer, Jun., was a volunteer in Arnold's expedition to Quebec, and died on the march."[86]

Daniel C. Bartlett was the son of a Congregational minister, who on the breaking out of the war gave him on the Sabbath his sword, which he had newly ground, and told him to go and defend his country. Mr. Bartlett went with Montgomery to Quebec, and was at the capture of Fort St. John, in Nov. 1775. He was also present at the burning of Danbury in 1777.

Increase Child, who lived in the southeast part of town, was a Captain in the Continental troops.

Joseph Mitchell was a private in the regulars.

Jesse Pennoyer enlisted during the war at the age of sixteen.

Jabez Flint entered the service at the beginning of the war and joined the army near Boston. His next service was near New York, when the retreat was made from Long Island, and his company escaped with peril from Governor's Island. In 1777, he entered the regular army for three years, and went to Philadelphia, and the next winter he experienced the sufferings of Valley Forge. Afterwards he became Assistant in the Quarter-Master's Department, and then Assistant in the Commissary's Department.

Judah Burton was in the Commissary's Department. Capt. James Reed was in the Commissary's Department temporarily; so also was Capt. Delamater.

Samuel Gray was in the regular army through the war, and had the reputation of a good soldier. He lost his life, in 1826, by falling into a

---

85 This was the most perilous year of the war for Dutchess county. The enemy were threatening the passes of the Highlands on the south, their armed vessels moved up the Hudson, and Burgoyne's army moved slowly from the north. Our Militia were called at times in both directions to meet the invasion.

86 Sedgwick's "History of Sharon."

well.[87]

Capt. William Chamberlain was at the battle of Bennington, and with him was Mackey, a small colored man, who had been a slave and gained his freedom by his patriotic services. He lived near Amenia Union in his little home, which was also given him for his service.

Garret Winegar was a Forage Master, and died before the close of the war.

Silas Ray was in the Continentals, perhaps in the Artillery. He lived on the road that leads to Kent.

Dr. Reuben Allerton was Surgeon at Saratoga, and as he used to say, "dressed the wounds of friend and foe."

Ephraim Lord was much of the time absent in the army, and his energetic wife managed his estate well in his absence.

Bezaleel Rudd, from the north part of the town, went with Ethan Allen.

David Doty was a very active officer, and somewhat restless. He was transferred, as we see in another place, from the Litchfield county Regiment.

Jeduthan Gray and Amos Pennoyer are honorably mentioned.

Capt. Elisha Barlow was temporarily in the service.

David Rundall served in two campaigns, one north and one south, in 1775 and 1776.

It is understood that some of the soldiers from this vicinity were infected with that prejudice towards Gen. Schuyler, which was so unjust to that excellent officer and pure patriot, and which was soon after happily removed.

Jones Knapp, who lived many years at Ebenezer Hurd's, was in the regular army through the war; was present at the execution of André; was at the capture of Cornwallis, and on his way returning from the south, visited Mount Vernon.

Warum Kingsley? Doubtful. He was very young. But he was present at the Massacre of Wyoming.

Some of those whose names are given in the preceding columns were in the service only temporarily.[88]

---

87 "Little Sam Gray would have another shot," said one of the officers at the close of a battle.
88 There were undoubtedly a large number of privates, who went into the service from Amenia, whose names are not here, as there are no records within reach of the compiler, and he is obliged to draw only from tradition and the very meagre records of family history. This will excuse imperfections in this list.

JUDGE PAINE

Among the civilians in Amenia, who rendered valuable services in the wars, none were more worthy of record than the Hon. Ephraim Paine, who was a man of marked character in public and private life, and was one of the first to stir, by his eloquent voice, the patriotism of the people. He was employed from the beginning of the war – as the "Civil List" shows – in offices of very high responsibility and honor, which placed him by the side of some of the greatest men of the new republic; and he was equally ready to associate with his neighbors in the minor offices of the town. His incorruptible integrity and firmness were not the less heroic for being accompanied with Puritan simplicity of manners. Judge Paine was not ambitious of place – as strong men are apt to be – nor was he dictatorial; but he was disposed to be positive and uncompromising, which exposed him somewhat to the charge of obstinacy. He was very singular in the simplicity of his manners and habits, but not boorish, and his theory of the social and political equality of all men, which he held as a religious conviction, was expressed in a literal and extravagant manner. He held that all men are equal, there should be no distinction in dress or equipage; he wore, therefore, the dress of a laboring man in the halls of legislation and in the house of worship.[89]

It was an aphorism with him that "all men should be treated alike." It is quite probable, therefore, that there was sometimes a disregard of that respectful deference to men in official and dignified positions, which the rules of polite society require, and it was the magnanimity of his courtly associates that led them of overlook these outward faults of his character in their thorough respect for he unquestioned sound qualities of the man.

Judge Paine's religious character was evidently somewhat tinged by his sympathy with the Separatists, or New Lights, among whom some of his relatives were distinguished leaders.

It is unfortunate that the unselfish devotion to the public service and the purity in private life of this excellent citizen should be less remembered than his eccentricities.

Many ludicrous mistakes are told of, which resulted from Judge Paine's plainness of dress, some of which have been magnified and colored in amusing stories. He was at one time treated as a menial by the landlady, where he was to stay during attendance at court in Poughkeepsie. The only rebuke which he gave to the mortified lady, when she apologized for her mistake, was "You should treat all men alike."

It is an authentic story that a gentleman who rode in haste to the

---

89   His clothes were not untidy, but coarse and plain, the manufacture of his own household.

house on public business gave him his horse to hold while he should go in and speak to Judge Paine. It is also true that a gentleman was looking over the farm for Judge Paine, and found a man ditching, and asked him, "Where is your master?" "In Heaven, sir," was his ready and not irreverent answer.

Judge Paine's education had been without the aid of schools, but his mind was disciplined to a habit of clear apprehension and accuracy, which made him on many occasions in his public service a valuable advisor in matters of finance. It is proper to say that he opposed decidedly the financial policy of Gen. Hamilton.

There is a notice of his family in its proper place.

In 1785, Sept 25, a few weeks after the death of Judge Paine, the Poughkeepsie Journal contained a fitting eulogy, supposed to have been from the pen of Judge Platt.

Judge Paine was a member of the Senate when he died.

Silas Marsh who was called "Lawyer Marsh," was one of the most active patriots of those in civil life, and Mr. Samuel King appears to have been one of the wise counselors of the time.

There was evidently among the leaders in this town a high respect for the character and services of Hon. Egbert Benson.

INCIDENTS OF THE WAR

This part of the country was singularly free from any disturbance by the near approach of the enemy, or by any movements of our troops. The people here, it is said, heard the sound of the cannon at the battle of Long Island, and they saw the smoke of burning Kingston, but it "did not come nigh them." The nearest encampment of the Continental troops, at any time, was at Pawling, in 1778. In the summer of that year a large number of prisoners – mostly Hessians[90] – taken at the battle of Saratoga the year before were marched through this town on their way to Fishkill, where they crossed the Hudson. During all the time that the British held New York, much of the communication between the Eastern and Southern States was necessarily through Dutchess county. Several notes are made of the travel through Dover and the south part of Amenia by American and French army officers and others.

In the early part of the war, a man called at Judge Paine's in his absence, and was suspected by Mrs. Paine to be a British spy, and she persuaded him to partake of some refreshments, which caused his delay, while she sent for two patriots,[91] and caused his arrest. He was,

90 Some of the Hessians earnestly solicited the people to aid them to escape, and some succeeded and remained in this country.
91 The men sent for by Mrs. Paine were Elder Wood and Mr. James Palmer.

however, an American spy, engaged in his legitimate enquiry, and the Committee of Safety, who knew him, were obliged to use some deception in planning his escape, in order that his person and real character should not be revealed. He was sent under guard on his way to Poughkeepsie, but made easily his escape.

A young man, by the name of Samuel Jarvis, went from Amenia, leaving his wife and two children here, and joined the British army. He went to England after the war, married again, and continued in the military service. After almost an hundred years, his legitimate family here have recovered his estate left in England.

Resolutions calling out the Militia of Westchester, Dutchess, and Albany. In Convention of Representatives of State of New York

Fishkill, Dec. 21, 1776.

"Whereas, It appears highly probable that the enemy's army mediate an attack upon the passes of the Highland on the east side of the Hudson River, and the term of enlistment of the Militia under the command of Gen. Clinton expires on the first of this month, and,

Whereas, His Excellency Gen. Washington has warmly recommended to this State to exert themselves in procuring temporary supplies of Militia.

Resolved, That the whole Militia of Westchester, Dutchess, and part of Albany be forthwith marched to North Castle, in Westchester county, well equipped with arms and ammunition, and furnished with six days' provisions, and blankets, and a pot or camp kettle to every six men, except such persons as the field officers shall judge cannot be called into service without greatly distressing their families, or who may be actually engaged in the manufacture of saltpetre, or of shoes and clothing for the army.

Resolved, that Militia be allowed Continental pay rations, and that such men that cannot furnish themselves with arms shall be supplied from the public stores."

The commanders of regiments were empowered to hire or impress as many teams as were necessary for transportation of baggage.

Commissary-Gen. Trumbull was notified to make timely provision for the subsistence of said Militia.

Col. Chevers, Commissary of Ordnance, was applied to for a loan of small arms for those destitute.

THE TORIES OF DUTCHESS COUNTY

In 1777, while Burgoyne was threatening the northern part of the State, a considerable body of the Tories of Dutchess county were collected at Washington Hollow, and made a formidable demonstration of their hostility. "An expedition was immediately set on foot to break up the gang." A company of fifty or sixty started from Sharon, Conn., and was joined on the way by others till the party amounted to two hundred. They halted for the night a little north of the Hollow, and in the morning made an attack upon the Tories, who fled and as many as could made their escape. Thirty or forty of them were made prisoners, and were sent to Exeter, in New Hampshire, where they were kept in close confinement for two years. No more trouble was made by the Tories here during the war.[92]

ROBBERIES

In the disturbed condition of society, incident to the war, lawless and rapacious men used the opportunity to indulge their spite, or to gratify their greed in plunder. In the near vicinity of the armies, and particularly on the "neutral ground," the losses of the inhabitants, and the dangerous annoyances, which were endured from marauding parties were terrible, and even in this safe retreat, there were instances of robbery.

Philip Nase, Sen., and his wife, who lived where their son, Cornelius, afterwards had his house,[93] had lain up and secured in a treasure chest a considerable sum of gold and silver money, and other valuable treasures. Four men in the disguise of British officers and soldiers, came one evening, armed with axes, and demanded the key to their treasure, and threatening death to the family on any resistance. The key was surrendered, and every part of the treasure was carried off, and never recovered or heard from again. It is not believed that the robbers were British officers and soldiers, who would not have been armed with axes on such an expedition.

The oldest son of Philip Nase, Sen., Henry, was a Tory of so positive a character that he left the country, and made his home in Nova Scotia. It is said that, before he left, he had concealed in some haste, in the night, at the foot of the mountain, a sum of money – eighteen hundred dollars in silver. When he returned to take it away, he was not able to find the place, and it is supposed to be there, perhaps, to this day.

The attempted robbery of Capt. David Collin, father of the late Capt. James Collin, came to a different sequel from the other. A company of robbers, supposed to be some well-known Tories, came to Mr. Collin's house, in the absence of his wife, and demanded his money and other treasures, which they probably knew he possessed. Upon Mr. Collin's

---

92 Sedgwick's "History of Sharon."
93 The house where Mr. Nase lived, and where the robbery was committed, was on the opposite side of the highway from the house now there, and was removed many years ago.

persistent refusal to give up his treasure, or reveal the place of its hiding, the miscreants proceeded to hang him, and would probably have carried their purpose to a fatal issue, but for the timely coming of his wife, who saved his life and their treasure.

The name of this heroic wife was Esther Gillett Collin. It is understood that the family have some memorandum of this event, and of treasures concealed.

The Baptist Church (built 1851; first edifice
near Red Meeting House, c. 1823) *AHS*

Delavergne Hill & the Dutchess Turnpike (constructed 1805) *GT*

The Smithfield Church (built 1847; first church on this site c. 1750) *RR*

Smithfield Valley and Smithfield Cemetery *(DR)*

The South Amenia Presbyterian Church (built 1881; first edifice was
the Round Top Meeting House at Amenia Union, c. 1755) *GT*

Webutuck Mill at South Amenia
(built 1846; site of 1st mill, built c. 1755) *AHS*

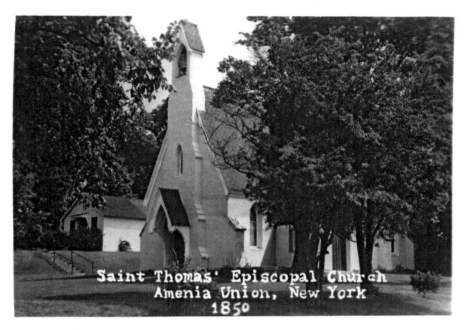

St. Thomas Episcopal Church of Amenia Union (built 1850) *GT*

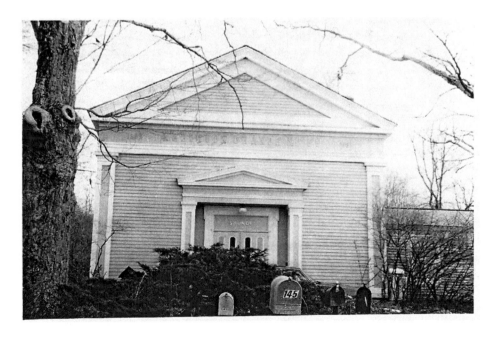

Methodist-Episcopal Church, Amenia Union, (built 1860) *AHS*

EARLY RESIDENTS OF AMENIA

These are arranged in alphabetical order, for the convenience of the compiler and of the reader.

This is not intended to be a genealogy of the families of Amenia. One or two generations beside the first settlers are in some cases mentioned, only to indicate their relation to present families. The records of genealogy, that valuable and interesting branch of history, are very properly made by many families for themselves. It is consistent with the plan of this work to leave out everything, with few exceptions, that does not belong to the early history of the town.[94] Of a large number of the early residents, no records can be found but their names.

Elisha Adams was the proprietor of "Adams Mill,"[95] in the west part of town. The right to the mill privileges and to raise water without limit was ceded to him by Judge Johnson. He was the first white settler on N. P. Lot 32, west of the mountain. Some of the family have remained in that place till within a few years.

Abraham Adams, Jun., is mentioned in 1765.

Darius Adams, 1765; Joseph Adams, 1762; John Adams, 1757.

James Allsworth, Jun., lived in the northeast part of the town.

Isaac Allerton, of Windham, Conn., purchased the farm of Abner Gillett – now the James farm – in 1787. Mrs. James was his daughter, and his sons were **Jonathan, David and Reuben.** Jonathan preceded his father, and was a resident of Amenia in 1775. His wife was Bathsheba Mead. David was the father of **Archibald and Isaac**, and his wife was a Montgomery, a relative of Gen. Montgomery. **Dr. Reuben Allerton**, preceded his father here a few years, and commenced the practice of medicine about 1778, first at Amenia Centre, and in 1785 he removed to Oblong, where he lived a while in the John Reed house, and afterwards till his death close by the Presbyterian church – now of South Amenia. It was probably immediately after the completion of his medical studies that he entered the service as Surgeon in Col. Hopkins' regiment, which was in 1777. **Dr. Allerton** was of a genial, pleasant humor, and very spicy wit. He died in 1806, aged 54. His wife was the daughter of James Atherton. The family was descended in direct line from Isaac Allerton of the May Flower. Dr. Allerton's son, **Samuel**, and his daughter, **Amaryllis**, are now living at an advanced age.[96]

---

94 These notices of families are put in as few words as possible; and the plan of making the work as condensed as consistent with completeness is sufficient apology for any want of smoothness of style.

95 This mill was burned, and another one, now remaining, was built in its place.

96 Dr. Cornelius Allerton and Milton Allerton were his sons. Mrs. Thos. Barlow and Mrs. Taber Belden were his daughters.

Rodger Andrews lived in the south part of the town, near Seth Swift's, where he reared a large family.

James Atherton, from Canterbury, Conn., was a resident of Sharon, where Zalmon Hunt now lives; then went to New Jersey, and thence removed to Amenia, where he died. He was a gentleman of excellent learning, and had spent some time as a teacher in North Carolina, and returned from there on account of his intolerant hatred of slavery.

Cornelius Atherton, son of James, was an iron manufacturer, and had a contract with the government in the war to make firearms for the soldiers. He removed in the early part of the war to Wyoming, and was there with his family at the time of the massacre, and escaped with them with very great difficulty.

Willliam Balis, Esq. was the father of the late **Abiah P. Balis**.

Col. William Barker was the father of the late **John Barker**, and lived on the same farm. He served the town in several civil offices, and was active in the military in the Revolution, and served also in the Legislature, as recorded in its place. His wife was Chloe, daughter of Mr. John Bronson, and they were married in 1763.

Deacon Moses Barlow and his brother, **Nathan**, came from Sandwich (or Cape Cod), in 1756, and purchased of Meltiah Lothrop the farm afterwards the home of the Swifts, and which they exchanged for the one where **Moses Barlow** settled, and which is still held, a part of it, by his grandson, **Franklin Barlow**.[97] Their father, **Peleg Barlow**, came with them at the age of 67, and died in 1759. **Moses Barlow** was the father of **Elisha and Thomas** and several daughters. **Hon. Elisha Barlow** occupied several important public trusts, — as shown by the "Civil List" – and was honored for his integrity and firmness, and was a gentleman of dignified manners. He had a numerous family. His oldest son, Thomas, was the father of **Hon. Thomas Barlow**, of Madison county. **Peleg, Moses, John, Obed, Elisha, and Jesse Barlow** were sons of **Judge Barlow**. The Barlows, before they left the Cape, had been seafaring men, and in an experience of the perils of their business, resolved to place their fortunes on solid ground, and this led them to their new home. They came by water to Poughkeepsie, and there has been to this time a grateful recognition by the family of hospitalities received at the Newcombs in Pleasant Valley on their journey here. (How many pleasing episodes would be revealed by the diaries kept by any other of these families in their interesting journeys to their new homes.)

Daniel C. Bartlett, from Redding, Conn., bought of Joel Gillett, in 1803, the farm now owned by his grandson, **W.S. Bartlett**. His heroic

---

97 The Barlow farm was on the "Clapp Patent," Oblong Lot No. 47, and was purchased of Mr. Samuel Judson.

conduct in the war is mentioned in its proper place. He was the father of **William and Collins Bartlett**, and his daughters were Mrs. John Barker, Mrs. Thomas Paine, and Mrs. Wm. Paine.

Zerah Beach, Esq., resided a few years near South Amenia, where he was engaged in trade about 1790. He was one of the leaders at Wyoming, who signed the articles of capitulation. One of his daughters was the wife of James Warren. It was his grandson who was the plantiff's lawyer in the great trial at Brooklyn of Tilton against Beecher.

Elihu Beardsley, from New Milford, was living in the Dr. Leonard house, near George Swift's in 1773. He was a tanner. His wife was the daughter of Joseph Chamberlain.

About 1743, **Silas Belden**, of Wethersfield,[98] Conn., settled near the foot of Plymouth Hill, on a large tract of land which his father purchased in New York,[99] and which was described afterwards as situated in Charlotte and Amenia Precincts. The sons of Silas Belden were **Silas, Jun., and Lawrence. Joseph Belden** was the son of **Silas, Jr.**, and was the father of **Taber Belden**, whose home in the south part of town is now occupied by his son. The land of Taber Belden was formerly part of the Knickerbacker farm. **Taber Belden** was twice a member of the Legislature, and very often served the public as a wise counselor.

Ebenezer Benham was one of the early settlers on Tower Hill, which is in the southwest corner of the town.

Bela E. Benjamin, the father of **Mrs. C. Wesley Powers, Elijah Park Benjamin and Horatio N. Benjamin**, married Louisa, daughter of Elijah Park.

Joseph Benson was an early resident of the south part of town, where the family have remained in considerable numbers.

Caleb Benton, of Guilford, Conn., purchased of Capt. Lasell, in 1794, the place now owned by his grandson, **Myron B. Benton**. He was the father of **Joel and William**. The immigrant ancestor of Mr. Benton, one of the first settlers of Guilford, who were, most of them, from the agricultural county of Kent, in England, and were noted for the very neat style of their farming. Mr. Benton left Guilford, because of the very inconvenient divisions of his land there.[100] He paid for his land here 15 or 16 dollars per acre in specie, which he brought with him on horseback. When the family removed they came to Poughkeepsie by water in a sloop. **Joel Benton, Esq.**, was much occupied in public business,

98 The ancestor of Mr. Belden was one of the early settlers of the ancient town of Wethersfield, and we find Deacon Joseph Belden a leading man there in 1706.
99 Mr. Belden purchased this valuable tract of land when in New York, and without seeing it. It remains most of it in possession of the family.
100 The farm lands in the southern part of Connecticut are, many of them, very inconveniently disconnected.

and was four times elected to the Legislature.

Moor Bird was born in New Marlborough, Mass., in 1756. He married the daughter of Louis Delavergne, and lived where his son, the late **Henry Bird**, did. His other sons were **Augustus and Milo**. He was of the same family as **Rev. Isaac Bird**, who has compiled a genealogy of his family.

Bockee – Soon after 1750, **Abraham Bockee** came from New York, where he had been a merchant, to Nine Partners, and entered upon land purchased by his grandfather, in 1699, and which has been in the possession of the family to the present time. He was one of the Colonial justices, appointed by the Crown, as early as 1761, at which time he is mentioned as "a **Mr. Bokay**,[101] a justice of the peace, at Nine Partners, near a place called the City." The immigrant ancestor of Mr. Bockee was **Johannes Bockee** (Boka[102]), who came to this country in 1685, and who was of that "noble Huguenot stock, that has contributed so many families of worth and distinction." **Abraham Bockee**, who came to Nine Partners, was the father of **Jacob** and the grandfather of the late **Judge Abraham Bockee. Jacob Bockee**, a graduate of king's College, N.Y., was Captain in the Revolutionary war of a company in Colonel Marinus Willett's regiment, and was a member of the Assembly in 1795 to 1797, where he introduced a bill for the abolition of slavery in this state. His wife was sister of the late Judge Isaac Smith.[103] **Judge Abraham Bockee** held several honorable positions in civil life, as shown in another part of this record. Though decided in his political convictions, he sometimes resisted the dictation of his party, and followed what he conceived to be right and for the public welfare. **Phenix Bockee**, a brother of Abraham, was Lieutenant in the war of 1812, and died in Po'keepsie in 1814.

Some of the Bockee family went to South Carolina, and it is a reasonable supposition that the gallant **Henry Bouquet**, who was distinguished in the war with the Indians in 1763, was of the same family, and that he retained the original spelling of the name.

Captain John Boyd was of Irish descent — probably Scotch-Irish – and came here from Orange county previous to 1769, and he returned and resided there again a few years. He married the daughter of Esq. Conrad Winegar, and resided a little south of Amenia Union in a house, which he built – now standing – where he died in 1817. He was the fa-

---

101 Documentary History, III, 985.
102 Boka." This is the proper pronunciation and formerly the only one. This fragrant old Huguenot name should have its proper sound.
103 Jacob Bockee and his brother-in-law, Judge Smith, and Judge Johnson, were very intimate, and dined together once a week at each other's houses.

ther of **Samuel**[104], **Gilbert, David**, and others.

Edmund Bramhall married a daughter of Deacon Moses Barlow. He was a carpenter, and built, before the Revolutionary war, the Deacon Barlow house, now standing.

John Bronson was the father of Mrs. Wm. Barker. "**Deacon John Brownson** died in 1785, aged 85."

Noah Brown was the ancestor of many of that name in the north part of the town – now in Northeast.

Lemuel and William Brush, sons of **Reuben Brush**, from Long Island lived in the west part of town, not far from the City. **Lemuel** married Mary Perlee, and his sons were **Perlee, Jesse, Platt, John and Henry**. **Jesse** was an officer in the Revolutionary war.

Gen. John Brush, who was a lawyer in Po'keepsie, commanded the Dutchess county troops at Harlem Heights, in the war of 1812, and afterwards Major-Gen. of Militia.

Col. Henry Brush was Captain of Ohio Volunteers in the war of 1812, and was on his way to Detroit with 230 men, 100 beef cattle, and other provisions, and a mail, when Gen. Hull surrendered, Aug. 16, 1812. **Capt. Brush** had arrived at the river Raisin, and was in imminent danger, through the negligence of Hull to send a reinforcement, of falling into the hands of the Indians, under Tecumtha. When notified on the 17th by a British officer, with a flag of truce, of Hull's surrender of his army, including his own command, he refused to accept the notice as authoritative, and escaped with his stores to Ohio.[105] The compiler has been informed orally that Capt. Brush purposefully allowed the whiskey among his stores to fall into the hands of the Indians, which so demoralized them that they were unable to pursue the retreating party.

Jedidiah Bump, and his brother, **James**, came from Granville, Mass. They were probably of Huguenot descent, the original name being "Bon-pas," then "Bum-pas," and "Bumpus."

Mr. Bump owned the east half of J.H. Cline's farm where he built a house, removed many years ago. He afterwards removed to the farm where his daughter, **Huldah**, now lives, 1875.[106] His sons were **Roswell, Elijah, and Herman**.

Judah Burton came from Horse Neck, now Stamford, Conn., previous to 1762. His house, which he built, and which was afterwards the home of his son, **Daniel**, is the brick house, now the residence of Edmund P Carpenter. Mr. Burton's wife was Huldah Stanton, of

---

104 Samuel Boyd lived where I. Hunting Conkling now resides, on the land, which came by his wife, a daughter of Judge Paine.
105 Lossing's "War of 1812," pp. 273 – 290.
106 She died in February 1875, aged. 92.

Horse Neck. **Sarah Burton,** daughter of Judah, became the wife of Ezra Thompson, Jun. **Daniel Burton,** the son of Judah, was the father of **Abraham and Warren Burton.**

Eli, Isaac, Josiah, and Elijah Burton were early residents of the west part of the town, and near the City. **Isaac Burton,** a man of good estate, was a citizen of Amenia in 1751. He is supposed to have been a brother of Judah.

Judah Burton was an officer in the Revolutionary war, in the Commissary Department, and is spoken of as "Commissary-General."

Ezra Bryan, one of the true Whigs of the Revolution, and father of the late **Amos Bryan,** lived in the north part of the town where the family have since resided. **Ezra Bryan, David,** and others are of that family. **Amos Bryan** was member of Assembly in 1840.

The ancestors of the **Carpenter** family of this town and vicinity came from England to Massachusetts in 1638; thence to Long Island, in 1686. In 1752, **Daniel Carpenter** purchased land in Crom Elbogh Precinct, near Salt Point, where he died in 1777. His son, **Benjamin,** being excessively persecuted by the Tories[107] — which is in evidence of his persistent patriotism – sold his land there, and purchased the lands, which, with subsequent additions,[108] made in part the farm of his son, **Hon. Morgan Carpenter,** now of **Mr. Isaac S. Carpenter. Benjamin Carpenter** purchased also for his sons, **S. Pugsley and Daniel,** the Evartson farm in Amenia, south of the City, where **Daniel Carpenter** remained till his death. **Daniel** married Zayde Perlee. **Morgan** married Maria, a daughter of Jacob Bockee.

Rufus Case was a resident of Amenia previous to 1800.

Daniel Castle, Esq., came from Roxbury, then a part of Woodbury, Conn., some time previous to the year 1758, and settled at South Amenia, where he was keeping a tavern at that date. He was one of His Majesty's Justices of the Peace. **Gideon Castle,** his son, built a house, where the South Amenia Post Office is, and afterwards purchased the James Tanner farm, where he remained. He was largely concerned in the purchase and sale of land. Esq. Castle's daughter was the wife of Capt. James Reed.

Joseph Chamberlain came from Tolland, Conn., in 1755, and settled on the farm afterwards owned by the Nye family, where he is supposed to have built the house now on the place. He was buried near the

---

107 This was at the time when Tories of Dutchess county put on such a bold front, and gathered their forces at Washington Hollow. Mr. Carpenter was three times robbed by them.

108 These lands were purchased of Daniel Shepard, Moses Harris, Samuel Pugsley, Job Swift, Dr. John Miller and others.

Steel Works, in 1765. His sons were **Colbe, James, John, and William**.

Col. **Colbe** was the father of **Joseph, Conrad, and Henry. John** was a physician of acknowledged skill, and lived awhile in Po'keepsie. **Capt. William Chamberlain**, the father of **Oliver and James**, lived on the farm now owned by J.H. Cline, and kept a tavern there, which was much frequented in the time of the Revolution. He was in the battle of Bennington, Saratoga and other fields, and he with his brothers were very zealous patriots. The family possessed a large fund of pleasant humor, which is not yet exhausted.[109]

Solomon Chandler kept a store near Amenia Union, in 1791. He lived a while in the John Reed house.

Solomon Chase lived in several places in this town and in Kent. He married the daughter of Joseph Chamberlain, Sen. His son, **Stephen Chase**, was the only passenger in the celebrated wreck of the Albion in 1822. He was on his way to England to look after an estate. The Chase family are supposed to have some hereditary right in a large estate there now.

Capt. Increase Child, who lived near South Amenia, was an active officer in the Revolutionary war. He was the ancestor of **Dr. Joseph Child** (?). One of his sons was **Mark Antony Child**.

Ezra Clark was from Lisbon, Conn., and was the ancestor of that family now in Northeast. He was the father of **Douglas Clark, Esq., of Moses, and of Elijah. Major Elijah Clark** lived near the outlet of Chalk pond and died before middle life.

Peter Cline (Klein), a native of Germany, came here from Rhinebeck, in 1760. It is understood that he left Germany about 1752 or 1753. He was one of those called "Redemptioners," who paid for their passage to this country by their service here afterwards, to which they were bound by the captain, who brought them over. Some noble examples of honor are recorded of these men, in redeeming their pledge, and Mr. Cline's was a singular instance of scrupulous honesty, in that through the dishonesty of the captain, he was led to serve out here the time for his redemption, notwithstanding he had paid for his passage before he left Germany.

Mr. Cline bought of Capt. Isaac Delamater, where his great-grandson, **Edward E. Cline**, now lives, one-half of Oblong Lot, No. 49, for two dollars and a half per acre. He left one son, **John Cline**, who died in 1845, aged 89, and one daughter, the wife of Allen Hurd.

---

109 Daniel Hebard, John J. Hollister, and Samuel S. Winegar married daughters of Col. Colbe Chamberlain. The wife of Capt. William Chamberlain was Abigail Hatch, of Kent. His daughters were Mrs. Solomon Freeman, Mrs. Roswell Bump, Mrs. Archibald Allerton and Mrs. Gilbert Boyd.

Mr. Cline's was an example of industry, frugality and honesty, leading to thrift, and that kind of thrift, which tends to the elevation of character and social standing.[110]

Captain David Collin, father of the late **Capt. James Collin**, and others, was born in Milford, Conn., in 1734, and came to Amenia previous to 1764, where he acquired by his industry a fine estate. He was the son of **John Collin**, who was born in France in 1706, and who migrated to this country on account of religious persecution, and settled in Milford. He was commander of a ship sixteen years, and was lost at sea at the age of forty years.[111]

David Collin married Lucy Smith, and after her decease, Esther Gillett, who was the mother of **James**. He was a Lieutenant in the French war, and was present at an unsuccessful attack on Fort Ticonderoga. It was he whom a company of marauders attempted to rob.

Major Nathan Conklin, of the north part of the town, was from East Hampton, L.I., from which place he came here in 1781. He was a public-spirited and intelligent gentleman, and was frequently Moderator of the Town Meeting. **Major Conklin** purchased his land in Amenia of Brush.[112]

Capt. Benjamin Conklin, the father of **Dr. Ebenezer H. Conklin**, of Amenia Union, was from Norwalk, Conn. He lived in Sharon many years, and in the later years of his life near Amenia Union.

Major Simeon Cook was an influential citizen in the earliest years of Amenia Precinct, and when the war broke out, he was one of the first to put his name to the Pledge, and to give himself to the actual work of the war. His wife was the daughter of Ephraim Lord, whose house stood where the Seminary now is, and after the death of Mr. Lord, **Major Cook** came in possession of the place, and left it to his youngest son, **Col. Solomon Cook**. His other sons were **Lot and Simeon, Jun.**

Rev. John Cornwall, father of **Eden B. Cornwall**, was from Cornwall, Conn. He lived at the Separate, and ministered there, and at the City, and occasionally at the Red Meeting House.

The highway at the Separate is on the boundary line between Amenia and Stanford, which is also the line between Lot No. 22 and Lot No. 32 of the Nine Partners. There was placed many years ago near

---

110 The sons of Mr. Cline were Peter, Allen, Philo and Ebenezer. Peter removed to Otsego county. One of the daughters of John Cline was the wife of Asa Hurd. Another was the wife of Thos. Swift. Mr. Cline's wife was Lucy Philips.

111 A complete genealogy of John Collin, of Milford, Conn., has been published by Hon. John F. Collin, of Hillsdale, N.Y.

112 The late Capt John H. Conklin was the only one of Major Conklin's sons who remained in Amenia. The others, and the daughters, were residents of Poughkeepsie.

the Separate a monument to affirm the location of this line. Two stones were placed across, below the surface of the earth, where they might be found by one who was present.

Dr. Cyrenus Crosby was the successor of Dr. Allerton at Amenia, and was often in public office.

Joshua Culver was married in 1767, and **Joshua Culver, Jun.**, learned the tanner's trade of Capt. Wm. Young at Amenia Union. **Mr. Culver, Jun.**, the father of **Backus Culver**, established his business at Pine Plains, where he conducted it with success. The family have been much identified with the people of Amenia.

Caleb Dakin lived near Coleman's Station, where his grandson, **Amasa D. Coleman**, now owns the same place.[113] He was the son of **Elder Simon Dakin**, who came from the vicinity of Boston, previous to 1751, to Spencer's Corners,[114] where he organized the Baptist church and was the pastor many years.

Jonathan Darling lived west of Leedsville.

Isaac Darrow, Esq., owned the farm, afterwards owned by Eli Mills, Esq. He was the father of **Azariah Darrow**, of South Amenia.

William Davies was a resident of Amenia several years, and owned large tracts of land in different parts of the town. He came into the town when a young man, and engaged in teaching a school at the Square, and had his home in the family of Mr. Benjamin Leach, whose daughter he afterwards married. While a resident of Amenia, he built the brick house, now the residence of Allen Wiley, where he lived a few years and then removed to Poughkeepsie.

Mr. Davies was son of **Rev. Thomas Davies**, a devoted Episcopal clergyman, of whom there is published a brief memorial; and the mother of Mr. Davies was the daughter of Joel Harvey. **Gen. Thomas L. Davies** and **Wm. L. Davies**, of Poughkeepsie, are his sons.

Louis Delavergne came to Amenia, evidently from Washington in this county, while his son, **Henry**, was quite young, and became owner of the mill property and one thousand acres of land, which he purchased at a low price. He was the brother of **Dr. Benjamin Delavergne**, and was the father of **Henry**, who retained the mill, &c. It is said that the emigrant ancestor, who was of a superior family in France, came to this country in consequence of having been engaged in a duel.

---

113 Mr. Dakin was the father of Caleb Dakin, and of Mrs. Coleman, and of Mrs. Barrett, wife of Mrs. Ezra L. Barrett. Caleb Dakin bought his farm of Allen Sage. Caleb Dakin, Esq., of Northeast, and Simon Dakin, Jun., were sons of Elder Simon Dakin.

114 Spencer's Corners in Northeast, a little north of the old line of Amenia, was so named from Philip Spencer, Esq., the father of Hon. Ambrose Spencer, who resided there many years.

It was **Dr. Delavergne** who built the dam near the road to Kent. It is called to this day "The French Doctor's Dam," and the remains are there. The object is supposed to have been to flood the lands above in order to convert them into a meadow. **Dr. Benjamin Delavergne** took a prominent part in the beginning of the Revolutionary war, and was major in the Fourth Regiment of Dutchess County Militia.

Benjamin Denton, Esq., was one of the earliest settlers near the City. He was the son of **Richard Denton**, who was the fifth Richard Denton in the family in succession. The first of the five is without doubt the Richard Denton, spoken of by Rev. Cotton Mather in this history, as having come from England about 1640.

Benjamin Denton's wife was Rachel Wheeler, whose family was from Holland. His sons were **John and Benjamin, Jun.**

Joel Denton, the father of **Joel Denton, Jun.**, was a landholder in 1791.

Capt. David Doty and **Lieut. Reuben Doty** are mentioned in the military record. A large family of this name were residents of the southeast part of the town. **Samuel Doty** was Collector for Amenia Precinct in 1762. They were from Old Plymouth colony, and came to this town from Sharon.

Capt. Samuel Dunham lived on the Sturges-Sanford place, and had a forge a short distance south of The Narrows, using the water power of that small stream. He was from Sharon. He married the daughter of Ephraim Lord, who had a right in the ore bed, which furnished ore for Dunham's forge. This was previous to the Revolution.

Benjamin Ellis, from Barnstable, Mass. (?), lived in the Oblong, and was engaged with Capt. Reed in the manufacture of iron.

Stephen Eno, Esq., was a teacher in this town several years, and Commissioner of Schools.[115] He became a successful lawyer, and was a model for the accuracy of his knowledge and the precision of his habits of business. He was a gentleman of the old school, and died at an advanced age at Pine Plains, at the residence of his son, **William Eno, Esq.**

Jacob Evartson, a native of New Jersey, came to Amenia in 1762, and purchased the south half of Lot No. 33 of the Nine Partners,[116] about 1700 acres, and in 1763, he built a large brick house, afterwards the residence of Mr. Daniel Carpenter, about a mile south of the City post-office. Mr. Evartson's ancestors were from Amsterdam, in Hol-

---

115 Stephen Eno was Moderator of Town meeting in 1798. It was considered the highest honor to be made Moderator of Town meeting.

116 John Evartson became the owner of Lot No. 33, and sold the north half to John Clapp and Henry Franklin, and the south half to Jacob Evartson. – Lib. 6, p. 222. The portraits of Jacob Evartson and his wife are now in the mansion of the late Governor Smith, in Sharon, and show them to have been of fine personal appearance.

land, where they had for three generations held the position of Admiral in the Dutch Navy. [117]

Mr. Evartson, in the cultivation of his lands and his domestic service, had a large number of slaves. He conducted also a store at the City for several years.

In 1776, **Mr. Evartson** was one of the Deputies from Dutchess to the First Provincial Congress of New York. About 1795, he removed to Pleasant Valley where he died in 1807.

Mr. Evartson's wife was Margaret, daughter of Gen. Bloom. His son, **George B. Evartson**, removed to Po'keepsie. His daughter, **Margaret**, was the wife of Governor Smith, of Conn., and his daughter, **Maria**, was the second wife of William Davies. He had several other children.

John Farr was the owner of George Kirby's farm in 1787.

Joshua Fish, Jonathan Fish, and Peter Fish, Esq., were residents of the north part of town (as it was) and near the Bockee's and Bryan's. None of the family have resided there at a recent date.

Jabez Flint, Esq., a native of Windham, Conn., came to Amenia in 1781, to the farm where his son, Augustus, now resides. He had served four years and three months in the continental army. His wife was Judge Paine's daughter. He died in 1844, aged 88 years.[118] His military service is mentioned in another place.

Eliphalet Follet was a landholder in 1768. Married to Elizabeth Dewey in 1764.

Capt. Robert Freeman, father of **Jonathan and Solomon Freeman**, owned at one time, 1757, a considerable tract of land in the east part of the town.

Roger Gale resided in the west part of town as early as 1776. It was one of his descendants who went from this town, and founded and gave name to the town of Galesburg, Illinois.

John Garnsey, the father of **Deacon John Garnsey, Dr. Ezekiel Garnsey**, and others, was from New Haven County, Conn., and settled where the family still remain. He was one of those courageous and conscientious patriots that never feared anything but what he thought to be wrong.[119]

Elisha Gilbert was a citizen of Amenia in 1762, and held land near the Eben Wheeler place in 1771. **Samuel** was the father of **Medad Gilbert**.

117 Admiral Evartson – one of these – received a sword from the hand of William, Prince of Orange, afterwards William III of England, in testimony of his heroic and loyal conduct.

118 Esq. Flint's sons were Philip, Alfred, Morris and Augustus.

119 Peter Garnsey, another brother of John, helped to raise a regiment, and served through the war as Quarter-master. Another brother, Isaac, also served through the war.

Thaddeus Gilbert was a resident in 1777. **Eliakim** was the father of **Daniel Gilbert.**

Gardiner Gillett, Joel Gillett, and Abner Gillett are mentioned in another place as early settlers in Amenia. **Richard Gillett** married Nellie Elliot in 1766. **Joshua Gillett** married Mary Knickerbacker in 1768, and lived in the south part of town and east of the creek.

The **Goodrich** family was in the part of the town now Northeast.

Joel Harvey, Joel Harvey, Jun., and Obed Harvey lived in the east part of town near Sharon valley. It is supposed that Joel Harvey built the brick house, where Eben Wheeler lives.

Capt. Robert Hebard, from Lyme, Conn., purchased a tract of land (about 1,000 acres), lying in the Oblong east of Ameniaville, and including a part of Allen Wiley's farm. He was the father of **Benjamin, Robert, and Daniel**.

Deacon Benjamin Hebard was for many years a leading and valuable member of the church at the Red Meeting House. **Daniel Hebard, Esq.**, removed to Poughkeepsie. His wife was the daughter of Col. Colbe Chamberlain. His sons were **John J., Henry, and Edward.**

Rufus Herrick was chosen Collector and one of the Constables at the second Precinct Meeting. Stephen Herrick appears on the Town Record in 1766, and **Benjamin Herrick** in 1767. The family lived north of the church at the City, where they built the brick house, now Robert Hoag's. **Rufus Herrick** was an active officer in the war of the Revolution.

Capt. Isaac Hilliard, from Redding, Conn., lived at Amenia Union. He was the author of several political and poetical tracts. One of his political tracts attracted the notice of Jefferson, who sent to Mr. H. a complimentary letter.

Stephen Hitchcock, son of **Samuel**, settled first in Sharon, and afterwards where his son, Homer, resided. His brother, Amariah, purchased of Dr. Chamberlain the place, now the home of Geo. H. Swift, where he died. **Samuel** purchased near – a part of the same place – then sold to his brother, and went to Schodack. **Thomas** went also to Schodack. **Solomon** traded several years, — as early as 1800 — at Amenia Union, and the place was called "Hitchcock's Corner."

The family was from Norwalk, Conn., and had come to Sharon in 1752, and settled on the farm where the late **Southard Hitchcock** resided.

Benjamin Hollister settled in the east part of town in 1741, on the farm where **Norton Hollister** lived, and where the sixth generation of the family is now living (1875). **Benjamin Hollister, Jun.**, built, about 1775, the house near Leedsville, where his son, **Nathaniel Hollister** resided. The family was from Glastonbury, Conn.

Deacon Asa Hollister, a native of Glastonbury, and an eminent Christian of the Puritan style, settled on the hill, west of Noah Wheeler's place, about 1780. The family were at Wyoming at the time of the massacre, when his father and brother were killed, and himself and the other members of the family escaped. He was the father of **Rev. Allen Hollister, Asa, Jun., and Timothy**.

Ichabod Holmes was an early settler near the Square.

Capt. Stephen Hopkins, a grandson of **Edward Hopkins**, one of the first settlers of Hartford, and second Governor of the Colony under the charter, was born in Hartford in 1707, and came from Harwinton to Amenia previous to 1748.[120]

The part of the town where he settled was considered central. The Meeting House was built near his residence, on land given by him for that purpose, and the Old Burying Ground, which was also given by him, was near the same, where he and all the early settlers of that part of town were laid. His house was southwest of the burying ground, and was reached in later years by a lane from the highway.

Mr. Hopkins was the first Supervisor of Amenia in 1762, and was elected also in 1764, 1765, and 1766. He died in 1766, leaving six sons.

This was an educated Christian family. The distinguished part which they took in the war is recorded in its place. **Michael Hopkins** was the first Town Clerk, and served in that office till 1773, when **Roswell Hopkins** was chosen and served till 1783; and was also Supervisor in 1777 and 1778, and he served also as a magistrate more than thirty years. And all of them were influential in the church.

Roswell Hopkins' house was afterwards the Totten house, where W. P. Perlee now lives.

Col. Michael Hopkins died 1773, aged 39, and his wife died in 1771. She was the daughter of Rev. William Worthington, of Saybrook, Conn., and was the sister of Governor Smith's mother.

Roswell Hopkins, Esq., removed to Vermont and died in 1817.

Gen. Reuben Hopkins, youngest son of **Stephen**, died in Illinois in 1819. **Hon. Hannibal M. Hopkins**, son of **Reuben**, was living at an advanced age in Goshen, N.Y., in 1872.

The only representative of this numerous family now resident in Amenia is Mrs. Peter B. Powers, daughter of J. Milton Wheeler. Mr.

---

120 He bought Lot 32 of the Nine Partners, and took a deed on the north half dated 1744.

Wheeler's mother[121] was the daughter of Roswell Hopkins. Benson Hopkins Wheeler, also a son of Anthony and **Selina (Hopkins)** Wheeler, is living in Chenango county, N.Y.

John Hinchcliffe, who set up at the Steel Works the first carding machine in this part of the land, was from Saddleworth, Yorkshire, England. He retained in a very marked degree the colloquial dialect of Yorkshire. He was a man of intelligence and considerable reading.

Ebenezer Hurd, Jun., came here from Dover about 1794, and purchased of Judson the farm now belonging to Mr. Chaffee. The family was from Rhode Island.[122]

Asa Hurd was his brother, and Mrs. Moses Swift and Mrs Pray were his sisters.

Jeremiah Ingraham, the father of **George and Thomas**, purchased lands of William Davies in 1789. **Thomas** purchased of Evartson about 1772, and **George Ingraham** purchased of Davies in 1794. They were from Bristol, Rhode Island. They had a numerous posterity, who have carried a healthful Christian influence into other parts of the land.

Mr. Samuel Jarvis, of Redding, Conn., came to Amenia in the latter part of the century, to the farm where Hiram Cooper lives, and his residence was the old house near Mr. Cooper's. He was of an English family of good standing, many of whom adhered to the royal side in the Revolution. It was a **brother of Mr. Jarvis**, who led the British into Danbury, when they burned it, and who, after the war, went to Canada, and entered into the service of the Crown. Sturges Sandford, a son of Mrs. Jarvis, came to Amenia with him.

Samuel Jarvis, who is mentioned in another place as going over to the English in the time of the Revolution, married the daughter of Judah Swift, and was the father of **Lancelot Jarvis**.

Thomas Jenks, the father of **William and John Jenks** and others, was a resident of Leedsville and owned the old mill, built by John Delamater.

Samuel Judson, from Woodbury, Conn., father of **Azariah Judson**, of Hillsdale, first settled on the Barlow farm, and about 1769 he purchased the farm now owned by J.S. Chaffee. His grave is near the Steel Works.

---

121 "Selina, wife of Anthony Wheeler, and daughter of Col. Roswell Hopkins, died in Feb. 20, 1797, aged 23 years." "Hannah, wife of Cyrenus Crosby, and daughter of Col. Roswell Hopkins, died June 16, 1789, aged 21 years." Mary Hopkins, daughter of Roswell, was the wife of Daniel Reed, son of Capt. James Reed. It was Daniel Reed who built at the close of the war, in 1783, the house now owned by Amariah Hitchcock at Amenia Union. He was father of the late William Reed, and Mrs. Nancy Reed Jerome and others.

122 Ebenezer Hurd's wife was Rebecca Philips.

Simeon Kelsey lived at South Amenia, and owned the mill, which he sold to Capt. Reed in 1781. Some of his descendants are in Sharon.

Hezekiah King was one of the first settlers from New England. He built a house near Amenia Union, afterwards called the "Karner House," and died in 1740. There is a meadow near, called the "King meadow." The Town Records of Sharon have this entry: "**Deacon Hezekiah King** departed this life, Oct. 9, 1740."[123] There was no church at Amenia Union then, and Mr. King was probably connected with the church in Sharon.

Samuel King lived on the farm now owned by Mr. Wiley. He was evidently an intelligent and trustworthy citizen, and was one of the patriotic leaders in the beginning of the war.

John King was contemporary with **Samuel King**. They were here as early as 1762 (from Greenwich?).

Stephen Kinney, from New Preston, Conn., settled in the west part of town, near the Separate, in 1740. He was one of the first in the religious congregation there. He was the father of **Roswell Kinney, Sen.**, and the grandfather of **Roswell Kinney, Jun.**[124]

Elijah Kinney lived north of the City.

Ebenezer Knapp built a house at the Steel Works, and owned the celebrated orchard of Mr. Sackett. Mr. James Tanner's farm was part of the Knapp farm.

Herman Knickerbacker died in 1805, aged 93 years, and was buried in his own field, on land now owned by Joseph Belden. A large number of graves are there of former residents in that part of the town. Joseph Gillett died in 1770, aged 29. He had married **Mary Knickerbacker** in 1768.

Capt. Joshua Laselle was a resident of Amenia as early as 1769. He purchased of William Young the place now owned by Myron B. Benton.

Benjamin Leach, a tanner, resided at the Square, and built that substantial brick house, afterwards for many years a tavern.

Dr. Alpheus Leonard was the successor of Dr. Allerton in the practice of his profession. He was a man of accurate knowledge, and had a happy faculty of illustrating his lessons to his students in medicine, and others who came to him for instruction.

Ephraim Lord's house was on the place now occupied by the Amenia Seminary; and he owned lands in several other places in the town.

Dea. Meltiah Lothrop lived on the place which was afterwards the

---

123 This is the oldest obituary record on the book.

124 Roswell Kinney, Jun., father of George Kinney and others, near the Separate, was accidentally killed while in middle life.

house of Judah Swift. That is a part of Oblong Lot 45, which Mr. Lotrop and others had bought of Cadwallader Colden. He was the father of **Walter Lathrop, Esq.**, and grandfather of **Silas, Daniel, and Walter, Jun. Esq.** Lathrop[125] was a man of extensive reading.

John Lovel, the father of **Capt. Joshua Lovel**, from Rochester, Mass., came into this part of the country in1745[126] and settled where Mr. Geo. H. Swift now lives, and in 1770 removed to Sharon.

Silas Marsh, Esq., called "Lawyer Marsh," was the son of **Cyrus Marsh**, of Kent, Conn., and brother of **Mrs. Anne Delamater**. He lived some years near Sharon Station, and awhile in the Winchester house. He was an active patriot.

Nathan Mead, of Greenwich, Conn., was here as early as 1740, and had purchased the lands now owned and occupied by **J. Franklin Mead**, who is the fifth generation there. **Nathan Mead** was the father of **Job Mead**, and the grandfather of **Job Mead, Jun.** These latter – father and son – served awhile in the Revolution.

The late **John King Mead, Esq.**, son of **Job Mead, Jun.**, and descendant of Samuel King, was in the Legislature in 1844.

Eli Mills, father of **Eli and Henry** and **Mrs. Rundall**, came about 1784, from Wiltonbury, now Bloomfield, once part of old Windsor, and purchased of Isaac Darrow, Esq., the farm where the late **Eli Mills, Esq.**, continued to reside till his death. He was a descendant of **Peter Mills**, one of the early residents of Windsor, who was a native of Holland,[127] and who was also the ancestor of the Mills of Kent. The name in Holland – "Mueller" — has nearly the same signification as it has here.

Stephen Morehouse came in 1792 from New Milford, and purchased where his grandson, **Julius Morehouse**, now resides. The large brick house on the place was built by Jacob Bogardus, who had been some time a merchant in Sharon.[128] His sons were **William, Zalmon, Garry and Henry.**

Thomas Mygatt, the father of **Preston and Thomas Mygatt**, came from New Fairfield in 1772, and purchased the lands where he resided, and which are still in possession of the family. He was a descendant in the sixth generation of **Deacon Joseph Mygatt**, one of that company of Puritans, who immigrated to this country in 1633, and who came with Rev. Mr. Hooker and his company in 1636,[129] and commenced the

125 Esq. Lathrop's wife was sister of Stephen Warren.
126 Sedgwick's "History of Sharon."
127 H. R. Stiles' "History of Windsor."
128 Sedgwick's "History of Sharon."
129 It was that memorable journey through the wilderness of more than a hundred miles by about one hundred men, women and children on foot, which is recorded in the history of Hartford.

settlement of Hartford. He was a wise counselor of the new Common-wealth. **Thomas Mygatt's** father was a citizen of Danbury, and was distinguished for his enterprise and thrift. The Mygatts in New Milford are of the same family.

Alexander Neely was Post Master at North Amenia, which is now called Northeast Centre.

The **Northrops** were an important family in the town of Washington, and some of them were residents of Tower Hill, in the southwest part of Amenia. **Enoch Northrop**, from New England, was the father of **Samuel**, who settled on Tower Hill, on lands still held by the family. The sons of **Samuel** were **William, Samuel, Benjamin, Nathan and John S.** The burial place of the family is at Lithgow.

Sylvanus Nye, from Falmouth, Mass., purchased in 1774 the farm, which had been the home of Joseph Chamberlain, and continued to reside there till his death. His wife was daughter of Dea. Moses Barlow.

John Osborn, the father of **Isaac Osborn**, was a resident of South Amenia, among the earliest settlers. **Isaac Osborn** was a man of some reading and of unproductive ingenuity. His son, **Melancthon**, went into the war of 1812, and it is said, was killed in the battle of Bladens-burgh.

Capt. Nathan Osborn came into the south part of the town after the Revolutionary war. He was a Tory, for which his land in New Salem, Westchester county, had been confiscated; and he obstinately refused to take the necessary measures for its recovery, and died in poverty.

The family, in the time of war, like many others in Westchester, were several times robbed of their goods.

Abraham Paine,[130] son of **Elisha Paine**, of Canterbury, Conn., settled in Amenia 1741 or in 1742.

Joshua Paine, also of Canterbury, the fathers of **Judge Paine and Barnabas Paine, Sen., Esq.**, came in 1749, and purchased in the east part of the town on Lot 59 of the Oblong. He was a farmer and a black-smith.

Joshua Paine was nephew of **Elisha Paine**, of Canterbury, and cousin of **Abraham** mentioned above. All the **Paines** of Amenia and Northeast are descendants of **Elisha or Joshua** mentioned. **Ichabod Paine** was the son of **Rev. Solomon**, of Canterbury, and grandson of **Elisha**. They were all descendants of **Thomas Paine**,[131] who came to

---

130 Abraham Paine took the first steps toward the organization of a church.
131 Josiah Paine, of Harwich, Mass., has compiled a genealogy of the posterity of Thomas Paine, of Eastham, the immigrant mentioned in the text. Abraham Paine, Rev. Solomon Paine, and Joshua Paine were great-grandsons of Thomas, the immigrant.

Plymouth from England in 1621. Ichabod Paine and Ichabod, Jun., lived many years north of Wassaic, on the farm afterwards owned by Leman Cook.

Hon. Ephraim Paine was apprenticed in his youth to a farmer, whom he served with most exemplary fidelity. After termination of his apprenticeship, he made a voyage for trade to the West Indies and to Cape Sable, which gave him the means of a settlement in life, when he came to Amenia in 1753. The house, which **Judge Paine** built for himself, lately the residence of Milton Hoag, is still standing (1875), by the turnpike, west of the gate. The land he purchased of Timothy Mead in 1772. [132]

Barnabas Paine, Esq.,[133] father of **Barnabas, Jun.**, and of **Mrs. Bennet**, of Canaan, Conn., lived where his son continued to reside, which is the place now occupied by Stoughton Moore. He had a knowledge of medicine, and was called **Dr. Paine.**

Col. Brinton Paine, who is mentioned among the officers of the war, &c., lived near the City on the Sanford place. His relationship to other families of that name does not appear.

Abaiah Palmer, father of **Abiah W. Palmer**, removed from Stanford to Amenia in 1789, and immediately took an active part in public business. His father's residence in Stanford was near the place where Cornelius Pugsley lives.

Elijah Park and Ebenezer Park, brothers, came to Amenia from Rhode Island in 1768. Their ancestors had emigrated from England in 1635, going first to Maryland, and thence to Rhode Island. Their residence in Amenia was near the ore bed at Sharon Station, called the "Park ore bed."

Ebenezer Park removed to Binghamton. **Elijah Park**, who was a public-spirited citizen, died in 1795, and his son, **Elijah B. Park**, and his daughters, **Louisa** (Mrs. Benjamin) and **Olive**, died also in Amenia. The other sons of **Elijah** removed to Binghamton, where the family is now well represented.

George Park, Esq., brother of **Elijah B.**, is living in Binghamton (1875).

Capt. David Parsons was a gentleman of the old school in his dress and manners. He was of the same family as the **Parsons** of Sharon, who came from Newtown, Conn., in 1763. His house was on the east side of

---

132 Judge Paine sometimes preached in the absence of a minister. There is a reference in the old church record of some disagreement between Judge Paine and his pastor. It grew out of no censurable conduct, but out of a disagreement in biblical exposition too positively stated.

133 Barnabas Paine in a few instances spelled his name "Payen."

the turnpike, a short distance south of where the turnpike gate now is, on Delavergne Hill, and had some appearance of style. **Capt. Parsons** died in 1812 of the prevailing epidemic. His sons were **Joseph, Joel, Truman and David**, and he had several daughters.

Joseph Parsons was the father of **Warren, Mrs. Bird,** and several others. **Joel** was the father of **Mrs. Westfall**, who was afterwards **Mrs. Palmer. Truman** was the father of **Sanford Parsons**.

Nathaniel Peck, of Bristol, R.I., purchased the Wiley farm of Garret Row in 1795.

Jonathan Peck, of Rhode Island, was owner of the farm where Hiram Cooper lives, and sold it to Samuel Jarvis. He built the old house near Mr. Cooper's residence. His sister was the wife of George Reynolds.

John Pennoyer, of Sharon, purchased, in 1743, on the hill east of Sharon Station, on Lots 60 and 62 of the Oblong. He was the father of **Joseph** and the grandfather of **Jonathan Pennoyer**. Some of his land is held now by **Mr. Sylvester Pennoyer**.

Edmund Perlee resided at the City, where he had a farm. His father left France, when about fourteen years old, without the consent of his parents, and after various fortunes settled in Amenia. **Edmund Perlee** served in the Revolutionary war, and afterwards became Major-General of Militia, and filled several important civil offices. Several of his sons were in the war of 1812.[134]

Nathaniel, Thomas and Obadiah Perry, brothers, of Danbury, Conn., purchased together a tract of land in the southwest part of town, and settled there soon after the close of the Revolutionary war. **Nathaniel** was the father of **Henry Perry**, and **Thomas** was the father of **Thomas N. Perry** and **George M. Perry**.

Mr. John Perry was from Huntington, Conn., and was a relative of **Mr. Obadiah Perry** and others in the south part of town. His place of residence was Perry's Corner, previously called Stebbin's Corner.

Yost Powers[135] was born in Naumburg, Germany, in 1731. About 1752, he emigrated to America, and settled first in Rhinebeck, whence he came to Amenia about 1758, and purchased, at several times, the lands still occupied, some of them, by the family. His sons were **Jacob, John, Frederick, David, and Peter**. His daughter, **Catherine**, was the wife of David Rundall. **John** was the father of the late **John Powers**. **Jacob**, the son of **Yost Powers**, was a soldier in the Revolutionary war.

---

134 Edmund, Abraham, and Henry were in the service. Abraham was severely wounded in a battle on the northern frontier. The other sons were Walter and John.

135 "Yost" or "Joest." This name is now represented by "Justus," the name of some of his posterity.

It is said that **Mr. Powers** came from Germany in the same ship with Peter Cline.

Stephen Ray kept a tavern near the State line, west of Sharon Valley, in a stone house which he built. He was born in England.

John Read, father of **Charles** and others, came from Redding, Conn., in 1804, and purchased the farm near Amenia Union, where the old stone house stands, and where he died in 1821. **Mr. Read's** father – Col. **John Read** – gave name to the town where he lived, which was then spelled "Reading."

The **Reeds**, of Amenia, were from Norwalk. In 1759 **James Reed** was one of a company of Connecticut troops, who passed through the town,[136] on their way to Canada, to the aid of Gen. Wolfe in the conquest of Quebec.

While on their way the company received news of the capture of Quebec, and were ordered to return. **Mr. Reed** was so pleased with the Oblong valley, through which he leisurely returned, that he induced his father, **Mr. Daniel Reed**, of Norwalk, to purchase for him some land[137] here, which he did where the late **Philo Reed**, son of **James**, resided till his death.

The brothers of **James Reed**, who removed here a few years later, were **Ezra**,[138] who lived where Huldah Bump did, **Elijah**, who owned the farm which he left to his son, **Elijah, Jun.**, and **Eliakim**, who settled where his grandson, **Newton Reed**, now resides. **Mrs. Warren**, wife of Stephen Warren, was a sister of these.

The emigrant ancestor of this family was **John Reed**, who came from England in 1660. He had been an officer in the army of the Commonwealth, and came away at the Restoration. He died in Norwalk, in 1730, aged 97. It was that part of Norwalk called "Five Mile River," on the west line of the town. Here Mr. Reed prepared a room in his house, where public worship was held till the church of Middlesex was formed, now in Darien, not far from the Five-Mile River. He was a good specimen of the Puritan soldier, who held his sword in one hand and his Bible in the other.[139]

---

136 This company of soldiers came up the west road from Dover, and halted for dinner at the brook, which comes down from Tower Hill. Capt. Reed often referred with interest to that place where he took his first dinner in Amenia. It was this mustering of troops for that campaign, which gave the poet Young some incidents in his poem, "The Conquest of Quebec."

137 The land was 53 acres, which Daniel Reed purchased of Joseph Clapp, the original proprietor of Oblong Lot, No. 47, called "Clapp's Patent." Here the young man began with his axe only.

138 Ezra Reed and his family went to Hudson and Coxsackie.

139 His sword was preserved in the family many generations, and they have been a Bible-reading family.

James Reed married the daughter of Daniel Castle, Esq., in 1759, and built his house on the spot where James H. Swift's residence now stands. This house was removed many years ago, and is now a comfortable dwelling, a tenant house owned by M.F. Winchester.

Eliakim Reed's sons were **Eliakim, Jun.**, who went to Green county, **Simeon** who settled in Vermont, **Silas and Samuel** who settled in Ontario county, **Phineas** who lived in Hillsdale, and **Ezra,**[140] who remained on the homestead. **Eliakim Reed's** settlement in Amenia was in 1773.

Capt. Reed was a man of great sagacity and enterprise, and was very extensively and favorably known for his honorable dealing. He enlarged his landed estate, conducted a store, and a mill, and a manufactory of iron, and in the time of war, of steel. He was also one of the first in sustaining a religious society. **Capt. Reed** left a good estate to each of his sons and two daughters.[141]

Joseph Reynolds was one of the earlier members of the church at the Red Meeting House.[142]

Jonathan Reynolds was a citizen of Amenia, residing in the west part of town in 1762, and was chosen Assessor at the first Town Meeting.

Stephen Reynolds, the father of **Dr. Israel Reynolds** and others, resided a short distance north of the City church, previous to 1767, in a house still remaining which was evidently built before the Revolution.

His father was **Francis Reynolds**, of Horse Neck, and his grandfather was **James Reynolds**, who died at his house on a visit in 1767, and was buried at the City, at the age of 93. The ancestor of the family came from England in the reign of Queen Anne. **Stephen Reynolds'** wife was Rachel, a daughter of Benjamin Denton.[143]

George Reynolds, the father of **Jonathan P., George, and Joseph Reynolds**, was from Bristol, R. I., and brought in 1795, the farm of Solomon Cook, where **Jonathan P. Reynolds** formerly resided.

Philip Row, and others of that family, lived in the extreme northwest corner of the town, where the late **Andrus Row** lived.

Daniel Rowley was from East Haddam, Conn.

---

140 The wife of Ezra Reed was a descendant of William Hyde and also of Capt. George Denison and Ann Boradil.
141 The sons of Capt. Reed were Daniel, Reuben, Stephen, Elijah, Amos, Gilbert, Jesse, Jacob, James and Philo. Only Reuben, Stephen and Philo died in Amenia. The others removed to the western part of the state. His daughters were Mrs. Northrop and Mrs. Rose. They all left families except Philo.
142 "Ruth and Lidia, children of Joseph and Lidia Reynolds, were baptized, — 1752." "Israel, son of Joseph and Lidia Reynolds, was baptized – 1754."
143 The wife of Dr. Israel Reynolds was Deborah Dorr, who was a descendant of Wm. Hyde, and consequently her name comes into that remarkable genealogy compiled by Chancellor Walworth.

Bezaleel Rudd and Zebulon Rudd were in the north part of town, as it was; also Elijah Roe, Silas Roe, and Jeduthan Roe.

David Rundall came from Horse Neck,[144] while a lad, about 1770, with an elder brother (Jared?), to learn the tailor's trade. About the termination of his apprenticeship, the war commenced, and he served two campaigns. He settled first north of Henry Peters, and in 1795, he removed to the place where he ended his days. "David Rundall and Catherine Powers were married Dec. 30, 1778. – Roswell Hopkins, Esq." He was the father of Jacob and the late Col. Henry Rundall and Mrs. Mesick.

Jonathan Sanford was the father of George Sanford at the City.

Samuel Shepard was Collector of Taxes in 1764.

Israel and Jonathan Shepard were among the patriots of 1775. The family owned land now belonging to Mr. Bartram. Daniel Shepard resided near the northwest part of town.

Parrock Sherwood lived near Amenia. Asahel Sherwood was the father of Henry and William Sherwood, and resided in the south part of the present village of Amenia.

Elias Shevalier died in 1808, aged 95 years. He was a native of France, and came to this country when a boy, and was sold, as they called it, for a given time to pay his passage. He came to Amenia when just married, and acquired by his industry a good estate. He was a liberal supporter of the old church in its beginning. His sons were Peter, Elias, Jun., Abner, Richard and Solomon and he had several daughters. Abner was one of the deacons in the Baptist church.

The old brick house belonging to Hiram Cooper was built by the family, and the last of them, who resided in the town, was Abner second, who removed in 1832, with John Dunham, to Broome county. The name is variously spelled.

Bowers Slason kept a tavern on the hill east of Sharon Station, which appears to have been a populous neighborhood. Peter Slason lived in South Amenia.

Isaac Smith, from Hempstead, L.I., migrated to Amenia in 1757, and settled on the farm, known in the family as the "Square Farm," where he died in 1795.

His ancestors came from Gloucestershire, in England, to Boston in 1635-6, and removed thence to Hempstead, in 1639.

Mr. Smith was one of the Justices for the Crown before the war. He had five sons and six daughters. One of his sons, Hon. Isaac Smith, the late judge, became sole owner of the farm, where he lived till 1813,

---

144 Horse Neck – now Greenwich – was so called from a neck of land on the Sound, where horses were pastured.

when he became owner of the Johnson estate at Lithgow, to which he removed, retaining at the same time the valuable property at the Square. His sister, **Catherine**, was the wife of Jacob Bockee. Dr. John Miller twice married sisters of Judge Smith.

Judge Smith was very enterprising and efficient in promoting the interests of agriculture in Dutchess county, particularly in the production of fine wool. He died in the midst of his enterprises in 1825.

Platt Smith lived in the north part of town, now Northeast.

George and Frederick Sornborger lived near Northeast Centre.

Capt. Roger Southerland lived in the west part of town near Adam's Mill. He was the father of **Rodger B. Southerland**, who married the daughter of Israel Totten, and lived where W. Platt Perlee now resides.

Mark Spencer, who distinguished himself by his financial operations with the late Jacob Barker and Matthew L. Davis, lived with his father near Amenia Union. The family was from Guilford, Conn.

Thomas and Timothy Stevens were early residents of the south part of town. **Thomas** was the father of the late **William Stevens**, who removed to the western part of New York.

Judah Swift settled in Amenia in 1769. He was from Barnstable county, Mass., and moved to this place with his family by a team of three yoke of oxen.[145] He settled on the farm where his son, **Moses**, continued to reside. His son, **Seth**, built the house where **Thomas W. Swift** now resides, and continued there till his death. **Samuel Swift** and **Nathaniel**, sons of **Judah**, removed to the western part of the State. The son of **Moses Swift** was **Thomas**. The sons of **Seth** were **Moses, Henry, Eleazer Morton** and **Thomas W. Henry Swift** was a lawyer in Poughkeepsie. **E.M. Swift** was a lawyer in Dover. The others were residents of Amenia.

The **Thompson** family[146] came to Stanford about 1746, and some of the family soon after came into Amenia. Their ancestors emigrated from England in 1637. "Being Dissenters, they came to this country quietly to enjoy freedom in their religious principles, and to avoid the persecutions and exactions to which they were subjected." **Samuel Thompson** was a citizen of Amenia in 1769, and **Benajah Thompson**, who lived where **R.R. Thompson, Esq.**, now resides, went from this town to the Legislature in 1804, etc. **Dea. Seth Thompson** lived about a mile south of the City P.O.

---

145 Moses was seven years old when the family came here, and rode one of the oxen on the journey.

146 Enos Thompson Troup, a former governor of New York, was of this family. The birthplace of Judge Smith Thompson was at the Square.

Israel Totten resided where W.P. Perlee now lives. He began here as a laboring man, and acquired a good estate by his personal industry. His wife was Esther Warren, from Norwalk, Conn.

StephenTrowbridge, of Danbury – now Bethel – was an early resident living north of Perry's Corner. He was the father of **Stephen B. and Alexander Trowbridge**.

Stephen Warren was from Norwalk, Conn. He owned the farm of J.T. Sackett, and built about the time of the Revolution the house now on the place. His wife was sister of Eliakim and James Reed. His sons were **James, Stephen, and Lewis**. His daughters were **Mrs. Shubel Nye, Mrs. Bishop, Mrs. Munson, and Mrs. Ketchill Reed.**

Samuel Waters, Esq., was a Justice of the Peace several years. His wife was Eunice Atherton.

Capt. Thomas Wheeler, from Woodbury, Conn., settled, in 1749, on the place now owned by his great-grandson, **Erastus Wheeler**.

Capt. Thomas Wheeler was engaged in the French War, and while serving on the northern frontier was taken sick and returned towards home. He reached Fite Miller's tavern, in Columbia county, and died Sept. 1st, 1757, at the age of 44 years.

Capt. Noah Wheeler, the son of **Thos.**, was a positive, energetic man, and of stern patriotism. He distinguished himself in battle, at Fort Independence. His sons were **Noah, Wooster, Anthony, Newcomb David, Eben and Alanson**. They were all farmers and obtained good estates.

Col. Anthony Wheeler was an active man in political affairs during the War of 1812, and was also very efficient in his command of the 29th regiment of Militia.

Elijah Wheeler, the father of **William and Cyrus Wheeler**, was from New Marlborough, Mass. He died in 1774, aged 41.

Robert Willson (son of **Robert**) came from the north of Ireland, when quite young, and lived in Connecticut till his marriage, when he settled in Amenia, a little north of where his son, the late **Capt. Robert Willson**, and his family had their home. The wife of the elder **Robert Willson** was of the families of Hinman and Thompson. The ruins of the log house where he lived are remembered.

Capt. Robert Willson, Jun., was well known to the generation of fifty years ago. Reuben Willson was his brother.

Gillbert Willett was one of the Commissioners in the distribution to the proprietors of the Oblong Lots in 1731, and he became the proprietor of Lot 52, which is near Amenia Union. The name is subscribed to the patriot's pledge in 1775; and in 1794-1800, **Gilbert Willett** was a citizen of Amenia and a magistrate, and kept a store in the west part of town. These – two or three persons – are supposed to be of the same family, and it has been said, they were of the same family as **Col. Marinus Willett**.

Amariah Winchester, from Kent, lived near Amenia Union. Mary Follett, of Kent, married Mr. Hatch, and they went to a new home in the valley of Wyoming, and were there at the massacre. He was killed and this young widow of 19 years returned to her old home, through excessive trials and dangers, so torn and sunburnt that her friends did not know her. She became the wife of Mr. Winchester, and came with him to Amenia in 1781. Their sons were Henry, Milo and David.

The **Woolsey** family lived on Tower Hill. It was **Richard Woolsey**, a devout man of Mr. Knibloe's congregation, who expired on the threshold of the meetinghouse. He had repeatedly expressed the expectation of instant death.

Capt. William Young removed to Amenia Union from Leedsville, and set up an extensive tannery. He built the house which is part of the tavern, and afterwards built the house which became the property of Dr. William Young Chamberlain. **Capt. Young** was from Orange county. His wife was Helena, daughter of Nicholas Row, Sen.

MAPS

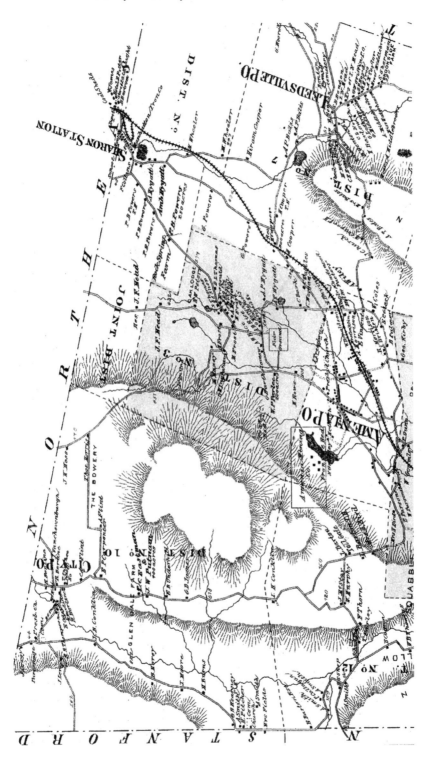

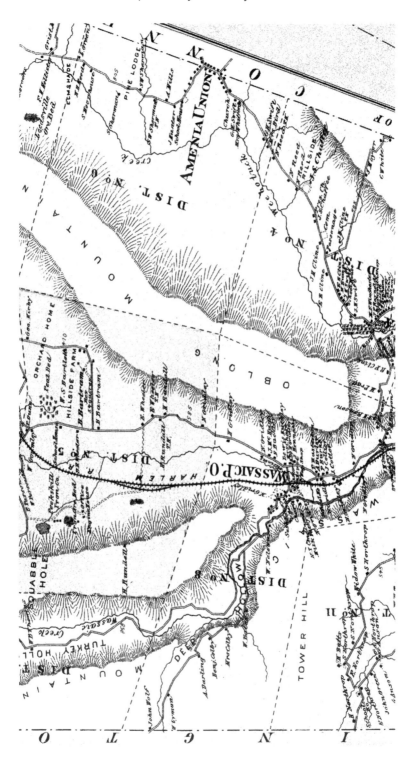

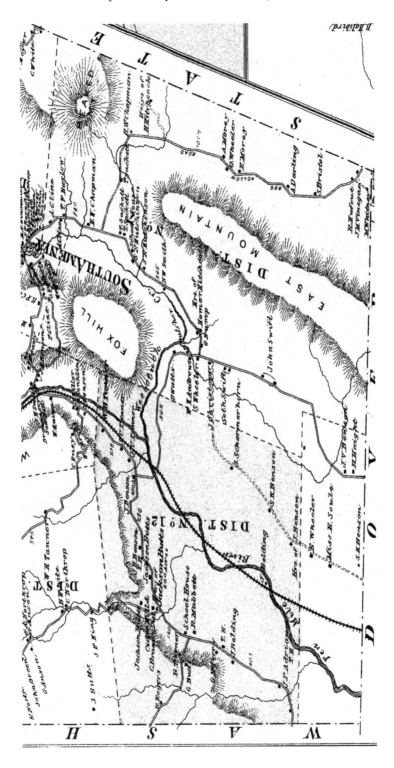

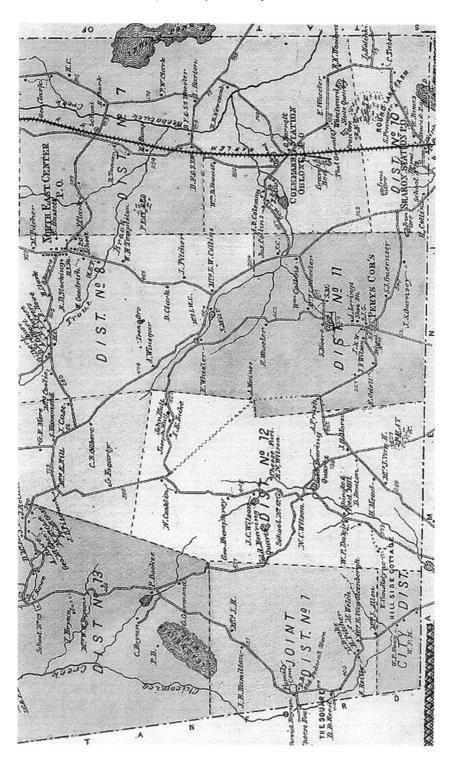

JUDICIAL RECORD

The Justices of the Peace, previous to the organization of the Precinct, were Castle, Hopkins, Bockee, Winegar, Smith, Garnsey, and perhaps some others.

The Record kept with admirable clerical skill by Roswell Hopkins, Esq., shows the "Actions determined" – civil cases – in his official service, which was more than thirty years, to have been 2,564. In 1777, there is a hiatus in the Record, which indicates partly the time when Col. Hopkins was absent in the war.

This Record shows us also the judicial penalties of that age, and it must not be entirely hidden that there were some convictions where the penalty was "lashes upon the bare back." These convictions were by a Court of Special Sessions, held by three Justices. In these courts we find associated Samuel Waters, Josiah Gale, Joseph Carpenter, of Stanford, James Tallmadge, Philip Spencer, &c., some of whom were from other towns. The fine for breaking the Sabbath, for drunkenness, and for a profane oath seems to have been three shillings, which went to the poor; and though the treasury was not much helped, these convictions were supposed to be a proper expression of public sentiment against the crimes punished.

March 24, 1784. – A man was convicted of stealing a horse, saddle, and bridle, and was "adjudged" to be whipt 39 stripes, and the court issued a warrant to Reuben Allerton, Constable,[147] who "immediately executed the same."

This is the only case in which the execution of the sentence is recorded. A part of the penalty in most cases was that the criminal be transported out of the county.

There is also a record of the marriages by Esq. Hopkins, which in 34 years number 182. Many citizens of the best social position were married by him – Daniel Shepard, Elijah Park, Daniel Hebard, Reuben Allerton, David Collin, David Rundall, King Mead, and others. It is understood that there was a peculiar grace of manner in the marriage ceremony of this Christian magistrate.

It will be inferred that this pleasant service was taken out of the hands of the clergymen of the town – only in small measure – when it is remembered that Rev. Knibloe in 26 years of the same period of time, married 320 couples.

---

147 This was Dr. Allerton, a very humane man. But such was the law.

SLAVERY

The German settlers and the Delamaters had their slaves, who were treated by them with exemplary kindness, and instructed them in the facts and duties of religion. Jacob Evartson had a large number — as many as forty - it is said. Several of the early immigrants from New England and other parts were also owners of slaves.

Most of the slaves in the town were manumitted in the manner and under the conditions prescribed by law.

In 1788, Ezra Reed gave freedom to his slave, Joel, and his wife, and their son, Jeduthan.[148]

In 1792, Samuel Swift gave freedom to his slaves, Pomp and Mela, "in consideration of their faithful services;" and in 1795, to his slave, Hannah, and her child, Zephaniah. In 1794, Judah Swift made free his "negro man, named York."

In 1794, Jacob Bockee gave freedom to his slave, "Simon Le Grand." It was very fit that Mr. Bockee should give this practical expression of his views on slavery, who a few years later introduced in the Legislature a bill for the abolition of slavery in this state. This important beginning resulted in the complete abolition of slavery July 4th, 1827.

They were not permitted to make any free and cast them off, who were not able to provide for themselves. There were, therefore, in 1824, a few years before the complete termination of slavery in this state, 32 slaves in Amenia.

"DUTCHESS COUNTY, STATE OF NEW YORK – This may certify that Joel Mandore, a negro man, formerly a servant of Ezra Reed, and his wife, now a slave to the said Ezra Reed, and their son, Jeduthan,[149] who is disposed to manumit the said slaves, and it appears to us that they are under the age of fifty, and of sufficient ability to maintain themselves, and of good moral character.

Certified by us whose names are hereunto subscribed:
ISAAC DARROW, ROSWELL HOPKINS, Justices of the Peace.
ELIAKIM REED, BARNABAS PAINE, Overseers of the Poor
of the Town of Amenia.
Amenia, Oct. 13th, 1788."

"Know all men by these presents, that I, Jacob Bockee, of Amenia

---

148 Jeduthan is remembered by some now as a much-respected citizen.
149 Jeduthan lived on the Darling place, near Wassaic, and became a respectable citizen.

town, in the county of Dutchess, and the state of New York, for, and in good causes thereunto, do manumit and discharge from my service, or that of my heirs forever, a certain slave, named Simon Le Grande.

"In witness thereof, I have hereunto set my hand this eighth day of April, seventeen hundred and ninety-four. JACOB BOCKEE.

"Witness, William Barker.

"The above is a true record. – William Barker, Town Clerk."

INNS AND STORES

It was the custom, almost universal in former days, in New England and New York, that the Inns, or taverns, were kept by citizens, who were the most wealthy and respectable of the people, very often by men who had large farms and possessed the means of providing ample accommodations. The public houses were not then, as now, located at the intersection of highways, and there was not in the early days of Amenia any village in the town to give local attraction to a tavern.

Daniel Castle, Esq., kept a tavern at South Amenia in 1758. Roswell Hopkins, Esq., was keeping a tavern when the first town meeting was directed to be held at his house in 1762, and the town meetings were held at his house in 1763, and 1764. In 1765 to 1773, the town meetings were held at the house of Col. Michael Hopkins. After that year – Mr. Hopkins having died – at Timothy Green's, Major Simeon Cook's, Capt. Platt's, Abiah Palmer's, and Capt. Wardwell's.

In 1764, the following persons in Amenia Precinct received license to keep a tavern – Samuel Smith, Robert Johnson, Jonathan Reynolds, Edmund Perlee, Stephen Ray, Widow Eunice Wheeler, Samuel Snider, Michael Hopkins, Simeon Wright, Stephen Johns, Ichabod Paine, Benjamin Hollister, Jun., Daniel Castle.

In 1790, eighteen citizens of Amenia received a permit to keep a tavern. Among these were Caleb Dakin, Abiah Palmer, Stephen Reynolds, Edmond Perlee, Jacob Evartson, Elisha Barlow, Zerah Beach, Noah Wheeler, Lemuel Brush, and William Davies. Some of these were without the obligation to provide lodgings.

One of the first stores established in Amenia was Capt. James Reed's, some years before the Revolution. It was a short distance north of his dwelling, and the place is marked now by a few locust trees, the offspring of those planted at the time when the building was there. This store was resorted to for trade by people from a distance and over a wide extent of country.

Stores were kept also at an early day at the Square and near the City, at Neeley's, at Delavergne's, and at Adam's Mills, and near the Red Meeting House.

The articles of trade were few, as domestic manufactures supplied so many of the articles now obtained wholly by exchange. Cotton, that enters so much into commerce now, was then scarcely known, and very few woolen fabrics came into trade — no hats, or shoes, or mittens, or any ordinary clothing. The trade was limited to a few articles of foreign manufacture, with tea, wine, and brandy, and the products of the West Indies.

Much of the exchange was by barter, very little money was used and that was silver.

Wheat was the first article of commerce that brought in money, first, by exportation in bulk by way of Po'keepsie; and after the mills were perfected, it was manufactured and sent in flour.

A serious part of the labor of every farmer and his team was the transportation of his produce to Po'keepsie, and the return loads of heavy goods, rum, molasses, sugar, salt, and lately plaster.[150] This burden is now exchanged for freights on the Harlem Railroad.

The people did not know the meaning of bills, checks, drafts, &c., till they learned by sad experience the story of continental bills. Money was hard and heavy. Capt. Reed at one time, when he was buying wheat pretty largely, requested his neighbor, Lieut. John Boyd, to bring from Po'keepsie a certain bag of silver money. Mr. Boyd brought it on horseback carrying it before him, resting on the pummel of his saddle. When he rode up to the doorsteps of the store, an attendant lifted the bag from the saddle, not without some exertion, and carried it into the store. This is certainly in happy (?) contrast to the present convenient method of almost dispensing even with paper money, let alone silver.

---

150 It is not out of the memory of the oldest inhabitants how certainly at a proper season of the year the returning wagon brought a supply of clams. A large number of families of this town sent annually for a supply of shad to the East Camp, following the traditional trail of the German immigrants from that place, who were the first settlers here and who kept up the traditional habit of making an annual visit to their first home in America.

MANUFACTURES

LEATHER

The important business of making leather was conducted in several places in the town. It was one of those industries, which were, in their location and extent, exactly suited to the wants of the people, who used the hides of their own cattle for their boots and shoes and harnesses. They did not buy or sell to any extent. Their leather was in proportion to their beef and veal and mutton, and the bark for tanning was near at hand. The skins were carried to the tanner, and marked with the owner's initials, and returned to him after several months. Then they were carried to the shoemaker, who was often connected with the tannery, and the shoes were made to the measure of each foot. Or, more frequently, where there was a large family, the shoemaker "whipped the cat," (whatever that means), went to the house, and they made all the shoes for the family for the year. Other clothing also was made in this way.

There was a tannery at South Amenia, established by Joseph and Gershom Reed; one at Amenia Union, by William Young; one at the Square; one near Thomas Ingraham's, and several others in different parts of the town.

The trade of tanner and currier was considered very respectable and remunerative. The mechanical trades were all honorable.

CLOTH

The manufacture of almost the whole of the cloth for the people was in the family. The wool and the flax were of their own production, prepared and spun by their own hands, and dressed under their direction, and fitted to their measure. The need of a new suit must have been anticipated a year, and the owner must wait and work for it all that time, before the suit would be ready to wear. But it did wear.

Every neighborhood had its shoemaker, and tailor, and hatter, and other mechanics, and these were scattered among the farms, and were not, as now, clustered together in villages, or driven, as many of them are, entirely out of the country. This explains the fact that the rural population of the town was greater then than it is now, and also the fact that any given rural district was able to sustain a much greater population than in the present style of commercial life.[151]

All this wealth of home-manufacture is removed from the country, and the sustentation of the people comes almost wholly from the land. This, on a fertile soil and with high culture keeps up the wealth of the few, who are necessary to conduct the business of agriculture, but on an unpropitious soil, the people, without domestic manufactures and left to agriculture alone for their living, become impoverished, and the population declines in numbers and wealth. This is true of many districts in our country.

It was a notable advance in the use of machinery when Mr. John Hinchliffe set up his carding machine at the Steel Works, in 1803. Wool had previously been carded by hand, but now it was brought from a great distance to this novel and curious machine, which was the first in this part of America.

LEEDSVILLE FACTORY

After the beginning of the present century, the hazardous condition of American commerce and the high price of imported woolen fabrics led enterprising men to enter upon associated schemes for the manufacture of woolen cloth. The Woolen Factory at Leedsville was established in 1809. Rufus Park, of Amenia, and Judson Canfield, of Sharon, Conn., were the principals in the company. The name "Leeds" was suggested by an Englishman, who was engaged in the works, and who had come from Leeds, in England.

Peace with Great Britain, in 1815,[152] put an end to the profits of manufacturing woolens in this country, and the company at Leedsville failed. The property was purchased by Mr. Selah North, who established the business of cloth dressing.

---

151 This is verified by actual count. In one of the best agricultural districts of the town, we count twelve families, on contiguous farms, where the children – mostly grown to manhood – numbered 32. In the generation before this, the children from the same houses numbered 115, all of whom reached mature life, and half of whom attained old age. There is not in this district of about four miles in lineal extent any mechanic, but a wagon-maker, a blacksmith, and a carpenter.
Although the older families have sent their sons and daughters to all parts of the land, and have become greatly diminished in numbers, there are yet more than twenty families living on lands, which their ancestors held a hundred years ago, or more.
152 The bell of the factory was rung loud and long when the news of peace arrived, but it was the death knell of its prosperity.

THE FEDERAL COMPANY

In the latter part of the last century, a company was formed in the northwest part of the town, which seems to have been for the purpose of general trade. It was called the "Federal Company," and they conducted the Federal Store. Judge Smith was at the head and there were about nine other associates. About 1803, another company formed, including several members of the Federal Company, and with William Davies at the head; and freighting business at Poughkeepsie was part of the scheme. Previous to 1817, an association was incorporated, including some of the members of the former companies, and they also had their headquarters at the Federal Store. The first operation was carding wool, by horse power, but not succeeding at this, they removed to the stream[153] near Adam's Mills, where they erected a building for the manufacture of woolen cloth, and in which they used water power for the machinery. The late Capt. Robert Willson was President of this company, and they issued a considerable amount of small bills as currency. The business of this company was not profitable, and the property was sold to Lawrence Smith, who continued the work of cloth dressing.[154] These facts were received from Capt. Samuel Hunting.

IRON MAKING

It seems probable that the important business of making iron began in Amenia some time before the Revolutionary war, and when the smelting of the ore was mostly done by the forge. On the small stream that passes through the mountains west of Leedsville, and a little south of the gap, Capt. Samuel Dunham had a forge. The ore used in these works seems to have been taken from the present Amenia ore bed,[155] as Mr. Dunham had then an interest in the Nine Partners Lot 32.

It is also evident that there was a forge at the Steel Works as early as 1770,[156] and the ore for that also was taken from the Amenia mines.

It is not till 1825 that the important works of N. Gridley & Son, at Wassaic, were commenced. From that time the manufacture of iron and the product of mines have grown into large proportions, and contributed greatly to the common wealth of the town.

The Furnace at Wassaic was begun and built up by Josiah M. Reed, Lehman Bradley, Nathaniel Gridley, and Noah Gridley. The site for the

---

153 The bridge where this turnpike crosses this stream was called "Federal Bridge."
154 Associated capital in the manufacture of cloth has never been productive in this town. Some of our citizens were connected with the factories at Amenia Union, in which there was a total loss of more than $35,000.
155 In 1743, a record was made of a right of way to the ore bed, which Waterman sold to Samuel Forbes.
156 Historical Record.

furnace – a few acres – and the ore bed had been purchased by Elijah B. Park, and sold to the above parties for six thousand dollars.

In 1825, the youngest of these parties began alone among the rocks, with a single team of oxen, the construction of works, which have arisen to so much importance. It was not without some doubtful struggles against adverse circumstances that success was gained. But all these men took hold of their business with their right hands.

There was no house in the place or any building except the remains of an old saw mill near the furnace dam.

In 1844, the property came into the hands of Noah and William Gridley, and on the death of William, into the possession of the survivor.

The furnace was at first called "Johnny Cake Furnace," from the local name of a street in the vicinity.

The making of plows was one of those trades, which were required in every agricultural district. The plow was of wood, and the wearing part of wrought iron, the share being frequently sharpened by the blacksmith.

Moor Bird was a skillful plow maker, and made cradles also. The cast-iron plow was introduced in the early part of this century, and the first manufacture of them in this town was by Mr. Calvin Chamberlain, at the City.

THE STEEL WORKS

Near the beginning of the Revolutionary war, the importation of iron and steel being cut off, home manufacture was necessarily stimulated; when Capt. James Reed and Mr. Ellis entered upon the manufacture of steel, at the place which has since retained the name of "Steel Works," and they prosecuted the business some time with success. They obtained the iron for their purpose in pigs from Livingston's Furnace at Ancram, which was a blast furnace, and the first in this part of the country.[157] These efforts at home manufacture were considered patriotic as well as profitable.

---

157 Isaac Benton was a skilled workman in his newly-organized manufacture, and received a high compensation.

2. The price paid for coal was twenty shillings a load, but it does not appear how many bushels constituted a load. The price for carting iron from Livingston's furnace was ten shillings for twelve hundred, which seemed to make a load.

3. Steel was sold for a shilling per pound at retail; at wholesale it was sold for four pounds per hundred, and refined steel at five pounds per hundred. Captain Reed, in 1776, purchased Harris' scythes at 84 shillings per dozen, paying in steel, and retailed them at ten shillings apiece.

THE SHARON CANAL

About the year 1821, the New York and Sharon Canal was projected, and many of the enterprising men of Amenia took a lively interest in it, though some of the more cautious ones looked upon the scheme as visionary.

This canal was to be constructed from Sharon Valley, down by the Oblong river, and by the Swamp river to the sources of the Croton in Pawling, and by the Croton to the Hudson – or from the lower part of the Croton to the Harlem river. It was also contemplated that the Canal would be extended north through Salisbury to Great Barrington, in Massachusetts.

The preliminary survey was made, and about sixty thousand dollars was contributed. This money was deposited with a broker in New York, who failed, which discouraged the managers, and the scheme was abandoned for awhile. In 1826, the project seems to have been renewed, and a Report of the Canal Commissioners was made to the Legislature, of surveys and estimates by an engineer employed by the Commissioners. The estimated cost of the Canal to the Hudson was $599,232, and by the other route to the Harlem river, it was $1,232,169. This was for the whole expense of excavation, embankments, aqueducts, locks, bridges, and everything to the completion of the work. A survey was made of the ponds and streams, which could be made to supply the canal with water, and also an estimate was given of the transportation to be expected. We find no record of the project after this.

We find a curious statement in the Commissioners" Report, viz.: — "It has lately been discovered that Lehigh coal answers an excellent purpose in smelting iron," and it is estimated that in five years the transportation of this coal for the iron works in Sharon and vicinity would pay sufficient toll to maintain the canal. The survey established the interesting fact that the Weebutook and all its upper waters can be made to flow into the city of New York.[158]

Cyrus Swan, of Sharon, Joel Benton and Thomas Barlow, of Amenia, William Tabor, of Pawling, and Mark Spencer, formerly of Amenia, were among the active projectors of this enterprise.

---

158 In looking for resources for a further supply of water to the city of New York, it has been suggested that this stream may be required. Thw waters of the Weebutook in the south part of the town are nearly 500 feet above the tide. Here is documentary evidence that the project to carry the waters of the Croton river into the city of New York was first suggested by the projectors of the Sharon canal.

TRAVEL AND POST ROUTES

The means of travel and communication in the last century were in strange contrast to the present. There was not even a stage coach or a mail carriage known in this part of the country. The only post road in the State in 1789 was between New York and Albany, and the number of Post-offices in the State was only 7. It was not till 1823 that the Post-office at Amenia Union was established, and that was on a mail route, which extended from New Milford, Conn., to Pownal, Vermont, through Sharon and Salisbury, and the principal towns of Berkshire county. The mail was carried through each way once a week, most of the time in a one-horse wagon. Previous to that, the letters – the few that were written – were carried by private hands, and the newspapers – from Hartford and from Poughkeepsie – were carried by post-riders on horseback. New York could not be reached in less than two days, the journey there by merchants and others being on horseback. Heavy goods came by sloops to Poughkeepsie. The line of stages, which was run between Poughkeepsie and Litchfield, through Amenia, turned a large current of travel into that new channel.

The Dutchess turnpike, so useful to the people of Eastern Dutchess and Litchfield counties, was made in 1805, against the protest of some who in opposition built the "Shunpike."

There is a stone standing by the road, which leads from the Steel Works to Dover, and where the stream comes down from Tower Hill, on which is inscribed "183 miles to Boston." Another stone is standing near the parsonage in South Amenia, inscribed "35 miles to Fishkill," "179 miles to Boston," "29 miles to Poughkeepsie." These were set up in the time of the Revolutionary war, while the British held the country below the Highlands, and this was one of the principal routes between the Eastern and Southern States, by the way of Fishkill, where they crossed the Hudson. There were one or two seasons when the salt was brought from Boston by this route. Officers of the American army and of the French army passed this way between the Eastern states and the Headquarters on the Hudson. The Hessians were marched through the town on this road to Fishkill, where they crossed the river, when they were removed from Massachusetts to Virginia in 1778.

In the early part of this century, "mile boards" were placed along the Oblong road, which told the distance to New York. The one at Amenia Union said "98 miles to N.York." The measure was probably from the Battery, and by a route less direct than the present route.

AGRICULTURE

Agriculture was the chief business of the early settlers, as it has continued to be of their successors. The two objects, which induced their emigration to this newly opened field – as we have been told by a contemporary witness – were the enjoyment of religious independence and the possession of fruitful lands. They were not refugees from justice, nor broken merchants, nor bankrupt politicians, nor wild adventurers, nor rapacious speculators; neither very poor, nor very rich; every one of them expected to gain a subsistence by the honest labor of his lands. And this productive labor was directed chiefly to the cultivation of land and to those mechanical trades, which are essential to the convenience of an agricultural community. It was very attractive to them that the title to the land was without dispute, and it also seemed to many of them a healthful atmosphere of freedom, where there was no interference of the civil authorities with the interests of religion.

Much of the tillable land was easily cleared, and responded bountifully to the simplest cultivation. There was plenty of timber for building and all other purposes. The land was well watered with springs and rivulets, the larger streams for mills. The mountains and valleys were the same then as now, which made it a most natural expression of the poet, when he looked over the landscape, to call the name of the town Pleasant.

It is a reasonable supposition that the sagacious pioneer looked forward with hopeful prophetic vision to the days of agricultural prosperity, which were realized by those who have followed him in his labors.

None of the early laborers here failed to gain a comfortable subsistence by the slow and sure gains of the farm, and none of them gained extravagant wealth; and through the subsequent generations of the citizens of this town there has been a more equal distribution of the property among the people than in most other towns of Dutchess county.

The first product of the land, which brought any income, was wheat, which began quite early to be exported. Mills were contstructed, as has been stated, first at Leedsville about 1740, and soon after one at the Steel Works by Waterman, and several others at different places in the town. In 1760, Henry Clapp,[159] of Rumbout (Fishkill), sold to Thomas

---

159 Henry Clapp and Elias Clapp were sons of Joseph Clapp, the proprietor of Lot 47, called "Clapp's Patent."

Wolcott,[160] of Crum Elbow (Amenia, then part of Crum Elbow), a mill site, where the stone mill now stands, and Simeon Kelsey built a mill there. Capt. Reed purchased this, and enlarged it by adding to it the mill at the Steel Works, which he had also purchased. The mill of Lewis Delaverge was also constructed early.

The production of wheat was greatly stimulated about the end of the last century, when, owing to the disastrous wars in Europe, flour bore enormous prices. Large crops were raised here which brought in an unusual income.

After the wheat crop began to fail, attention was turned more to corn, and for a few years to barley, and then to oats. About the beginning of this century, the farmers of Dutchess county began to use plaster, and the cultivation of grass, which was followed by an increased number of fatting cattle and sheep, and an improvement of the land. In 1825, the production of fine wool became of general importance, and, in 1835, the number of sheep in Amenia was 21,761, and in Dutchess county 230,000. These statistics are given, only to compare the earlier with the later farming of these lands; and not to extend the history over these later years.

The price of wheat in 1776 was five shillings a bushel, and that was the price of a day's work in harvesting. Butter was ten pence per pound. The wages of a hired girl at housework or spinning was five shillings a week. They were not servants as a class, but were many of them equal in social position to their employers.

---

160 Thomas Wolcott, the father of Luke Wolcott, was a blacksmith at South Amenia, and already had a sawmill on the stream opposite the mill site.

THE WAR OF 1812

The losses of the people of Amenia by the utter depreciation of continental money was not so serious as to those in other places, as only a few here were engaged in any business that required much capital; but the demoralizing influence of the war upon society and the disturbance of industrial pursuits were manifested for many years, and it was some time before the business and social interests of the people were restored to their former prosperity.

It is understood that the people of Amenia took an intelligent interest in the great questions, which agitated the country previous to the final ratification of the National Constitution, and in all those national subjects, which awakened so much discussion and no little dissension previous to the War of 1812. All those differences of sentiment, which divided the nation into two parties, were sharply defined here. The embargo and the other restrictions upon commerce were not regarded as affecting their pecuniary interests, not being a commercial people but they took distinct and positive ground on those matters of national interest, which seemed to dictate a choice between the British and the French nations in any close political affinity. The voters of the town were almost equally divided on the questions for many years.

When war was declared in 1812, there was only a partial response here to the call for men, though there was no violent opposition to the measures of the Government. A few men were enlisted into the regular army, one or two volunteer companies were raised and sent to New York, and drafts were made from the uniform companies and other militia. Col. John Brush commanded the troops from Dutchess county, which were stationed at Harlem Heights. Henry Perlee was Captain of one of the companies, Jacob Rundall served as Captain, and William Barker and Samuel Russell served under Col. Anthony Delamater. Jesse Barlow was Captain of a volunteer company and was stationed on Staten Island. Archibald Allerton served as lieutenant in a company of light horse. Of others in the service, only a few names are found by diligent enquiry. William Snyder, Elijah Stevens, Russell Stevens, John Jenks, Elijah Andrews, Ashbel Porter, Cornelius Jordan, Isaac Latimer, Seymour Haskins, Alexander Haskins, Asa Hollister, Hezekiah Lewis, Eben Wheeler, Solomon Wheeler, Simeon Hall, George Reynolds, Jonathan P. Reynolds, Milton Mason and Enoch Anson.

Lieut. Obed Barlow died near New York of a fever at the age of twenty-one years. Lieut. Phenix Bockee was taken sick and died in Poughkeepsie. Sergeant Daniel Shepard returned home sick and died there. Colbe Chamberlain returned and died at home. The gallant conduct of Capt. Henry Brush is mentioned in another place; also of the death of young Spencer.

There was very great imperfection in the sanitary arrangements of the military service in that war, in very marked contrast with those of our own late terrible struggle. There was then also lacking, perhaps, something of that moral enthusiasm, which sustained the soldiers of this war.

It is surprising, that with such inadequate resourses, which the nation then possessed, that such important ends should have been attained in the War of 1812, which Mr. Lossing calls "the second War for Independence."

PROFESSIONAL MEN

There has scarcely been a lawyer in the town, who has made the practice of his profession his chief business, though a considerable number who were natives of Amenia, and received their early education here, have become eminent at the bar and on the bench. The people of Amenia have been specially indisposed to litigation. From the earliest history of the town to the present, they have been noted for their freedom from family rivalry, from a desire for pre-eminence in wealth and social position, and from ambitious ostentation, and for their mutual confidence and good will to each other. This is the testimony of an eminent lawyer who went out from them.

Barnabas Paine, Esq., was known as Dr. Paine, and he is supposed to have received a medical education, and appears to have been a man of considerable learning. But he was not at any time exclusively occupied in the practice of his profession.

Dr. John Chamberlain was considered a skillful physician, and practiced some time in Poughkeepsie.

Dr. Doty practiced some time in the east part of the town, and Dr. Delavergne, the "French doctor," as he was called, lived in the town some years.

Dr. Reuben Allerton was a thoroughly educated physician, and was engaged in an extensive practice when he died at the age of 54. His son, Dr. Cornelius Allerton, spent most of his professional life at Pine Plains.

Dr. Cyrenus Crosby was the successor of Dr. Allerton in the west part of the town, and was a man of excellent attainments.

Dr. Alpheus Leonard, from Canton, Conn., who succeeded Dr. Allerton in the Oblong, was accustomed to have under his tuition a class of medical students.

Dr. Elmore Everitt succeeded Dr. Leonard.

There has been since their day a succession of educated and skillful physicians in the town, who are remembered by the present generation.

LIBRARIES AND SCHOOLS

The people were from an early day in their history indebted largely to their public libraries for the high degree of intelligence which they attained. In Mr. Knibloe's congregation a library was collected at a very early period, which was kept at Amenia Union. After that a larger and more valuable library was incorporated by the name of "Union Library," which was kept at Leedsville. This was a collection of the most instructive literature in the language, and the books were read by a large proportion of the families in the town. Four times a year there was a "library day," when all the books were returned and others were drawn out. On these occasions a large company were collected to attend the drawing. A public library was also instituted at Ameniaville of similar literary works.

The common schools of the town were of an excellent character, and were resorted to by all families, where they received a solid, though limited, education, and there were some excellent private schools.

Besides Rev. Mr. Barnett's private instruction to young men – which has been mentioned – a number of private schools for young women were instituted at different times. Mrs. Knies, daughter of Dr. Thomas Young, Miss Neely, and later Miss Susan Nye, assisted to improve the tone of female education; and many of the youth of both sexes were sent to the best schools in New England.

It was not till 1835 that the Amenia Seminary began its excellent work. This was the natural outgrowth of a settled conviction in the minds of the people of the value of higher education, and the advantages of it have been such as might be expected to a people so disposed, and from the eminent character of the instructors, who have been connected with the institution. The advantages were not only to the families of Amenia, whose sons and daughters were assisted there in their qualifications for usefulness at home and for honorable positions in other parts of the land; but large numbers have come here from other towns and distant places for their education.

The alumni of this institution have carried its good name into all the land. The late Rev. Bishop Clark has said, "that in every one of his widely-extended fields of labor, he has met the students of Amenia Seminary, not only in the ministry, but filling their proper places in the other learned professions." And they all seem to cherish a happy remembrance of the scenes which surrounded them here, and of the incidents of their school-day life – associations which are never forgotten.

Some of those connected with the institution were the late
Rev. Bishop Clark,
Rev. Bishop Haven,
Prof. Charles K. True, D.D.,
Rev. Joseph Cummings, D.D., President of Wesleyan University,
Rev. E.O. Haven, Chancellor of the University of Syracuse,
Rev. President Merrick, D.D.,
Rev. J.W. Beach, D.D.,
Rev. Cyrus Foss, D.D.,
Rev. Dr. Kidder,
Rev. A.J. Hunt,
Rev. A.S. Hunt, D.D.,
Rev. H.N. Powers, D.D.,
Prof. Alexander Winchell, LL.D.,
and many others, both teachers and pupils, of whom it is too nearly contemporary to speak.

The present rising condition of Amenia Seminary speaks for itself.

THE "AMENIA TIMES"

It is not out of place, and, perhaps, not out of time – as illustrating the early tendency of the people of Amenia to intelligent study – to make this record, that the "Amenia Times" was instituted by the people themselves, and has been sustained by them as a necessary medium of business and literary intercourse.

The conduct of this journal, so long under the direction and moulding hand of one of Amenia's sons, has been such as to reflect the tast of a cultivated community, and its good name is cherished with a reasonable pride by the citizens of the town.[161]

---

161 The "Amenia Times" was established in 1852.

THE OLD HOUSES

There are only about ten or twelve of the old dwellings, which were built more than a hundred years ago, the few visible monuments of that period of our history. An old house is in itself a history. It seems to speak to us of the successive generations that have lived and died there.

The house of Mr. Nye's family is supposed to have been built by Joseph Chamberlain, who died in 1765.

Deacon Barlow's house, now belonging to Albert Cline, was built a little previous to the Revolution.

The house built by Capt. Reed, in 1760, now removed, and belonging to Mr. Winchester.

Mr. Gridley's Red House, near Wassaic.

The house which makes part of the residence of N. Reed.

The Capt. Boyd house, belonging to G.H. Swift.

The large stone house, built by Hendrick Winegar, in 1761.

The house of brick and wood, built by Johannes Delamater and Mary, his wife, in 1761, now belonging to to M.B. Benton.

Judge Paine's house, where Milton Hoag lived, which is almost ready to fall down.

The Evartson house, occupied by Mr. Putnam, was built in a superior manner, in 1763, by Jacob Evartson, and is well preserved.

The residence of the Reynolds family, north of the City church, now in ruins, is undoubtedly one of the ante-revolutionary structures.

Besides these dwellings, there is one edifice, which has outlived all memories, traditions and records, and that is the Old Separate Meeting House. It is evidently from its name – which points to a known period in church history – and from the absence of all tradition and record concerning it, one of the oldest structures in this town or vicinity.

It is the last remaining specimen of that style of church architecture, which prevailed for rural churches a hundred and fifty yeards ago; and although it was renewed and altered inside many years ago, the outward form is the same. It represents no Christian community, and is claimed by none. It seems to be purposefully forgotten. It stands as a significant memento of the time – which has come – of forgetfulness of old separations, and of all dissensions among Christians. Let it stand.

We cannot go and look upon those old dwellings without passing some of those older and more enduring dwellings of families; well-chosen places where with filial reverence they made the graves of their fathers.

That was a hundred and twenty years ago and more, and every year some have been added to that number, from successive generations, which keeps up the bond between the earlier residents here and ourselves.

Mr. Sackett was buried in 1746, the earliest burial here which is recorded. In that old ground near Amenia Union, so beautifully situated, Uldrick Winegar, the patriarch of the family, was buried in 1754, at the age of 102 years. Eve, the wife of Hendrick Winegar, died in 1749. The stone at her grave seems to be the oldest which is known in the town. There is a stone in the ground near Coleman's, where the Wheelers and Collins and others are buried, which is also dated 1749. The name on this stone is Ruth Curtis; and she was apparently one of the ancestors of the family of Capt. Thomas Wheeler.

The old ground at the City is still the burial place of many families there, although there are some private grounds within the bounds of that congregation. The old burying place at Amenia, which contains so many honored names, is cherished with affectionate care by the friends, though they have arranged with excellent taste a new cemetery for the present and future generations.

Many there are in these old dwelling places, who have no other written memorial than what has been read on their monumental stone, which affirms what has been already said, that the unwritten life of this people is immeasurably greater that all that is written or remembered of them.

But the brief lines in an old graveyard have an intensity of historic interest, which is not found in any printed volume; whether we rub off the moss of one hundred and twenty years, or pause over the grave of one so recently laid there, that we are unwilling to speak the name. We are touched with the very brevity of the record, cut in enduring stone, where it will be studied, after all these written memorials are forgotten.

THE END.

SUBSCRIBERS TO THIS WORK

These names are inserted in the book as part of the history. A large number of the subscribers have a hereditary interest in the early residents of Amenia, and many others have become intimately connected with the people of the town by their residence here or by other associations.

Adam, Wm.
Allerton, Archibald, M.
Allerton, David
Allerton, Mrs. Byron
Allerton, Lois
Allerton, Orville H.
Andrews, Mrs. Henry
Baird, Rev. C.W.
Barlow, Henry
Barlow, Franklin
Barlow, Jesse
Barnum, John D.
Barrett, Oliver
Barrett, Rev. Myron
Bartlett, Wm H.
Bartlett, Wm. S.
Bartram, Barney
Bassett, Joseph
Belden, Joseph
Bennett, John
Benson, Joseph H.
Benton, Charles E.
Benton, Joel
Benton, Ezra R.
Benton, Myron B.
Benton, O.A.
Benton, Simeon
Bertine, Robert
Bird, Milo
Bockee, Phenix
Bostwick, Charles E.
Bowdish, Mrs. S.A.
Bowne, Sarah E.
Boyd, John

Boyd, John G.
Bronson, Asahel, D.D.
Bryan, Ezra
Bullions, A.B., D.D.
Bump, Julia
Bumster, James W.
Carpenter, Mary S.
Carpenter, Isaac S.
Carpenter, Jacob B.
Carter, Frederick
Chaffee, Jerome S.
Chamberlain, Rev. Albert
Chamberlain, George
Chamberlain, Oliver
Chamberlain, Morton S.
Chase, John H.
Church, Wm. L.
Clark, Douglass
Clark, Edgar
Clark, Henry
Clark, Lorin
Cline, Albert
Cline, Edward E.
Cline, Franklin
Cline, J.H.
Cline, Mrs. Maria
Coleman, Amasa D.
Collin, Mrs. Louisa
Conklin, Amariah, M.D.
Conklin, I. Huntting
Conklin, Nathan
Conklin, Wm. B.
Cornwell, Wm. I.
Crane, George E.

Crane, Mrs. Munroe
Cummings, Rev. Dr. J.
Dakin, Wm. P.
Darke, Charles
De Lacey, Wm. L.
Demming, Ralph, M.D.
Denniston, Rev. James O.
Durant, Mrs. Harriet
Eaton, L.F.
Edgerton, Sheldon
Fitch, Arthur
Fitch, Rev. Silas
Flint, Augustus
Flint, Charles A.
Frissell, Rev. A.C.
Frost, Prof. S.T.
Frost, Hyatt
Fry, Simeon
Gilbert, Lorenzo
Gray, Frank
Greene, Louis C., M.D.
Gridley, Edward
Gridley, Noah
Griffin, Theron
Guernsey, De Sault, M.D.
Guernsey, John
Guernsey, Samuel
Hammond, John
Haskins, John
Hatch, L.P.
Hatch, Mrs. R.C.
Haven, E.O., D.D.
Hebard, George E.
Hebard, Newton
Historical Society, L.I.
Hitchcock, Amariah
Hitchcock, Charles
Hitchcock, E.R.
Hitchcock, Homer
Hitchcock, Solomon
Hoagland, A.R.G.
Hollister, Asa
Hollister, F. Reed
Hollister, Hiel
Hollister, Milo

Hope, Anna
Horton, Emily
Hotchkiss, Fred A.
Hufcutt, George
Hunt, Rev. A.J.
Hurd, Egbert
Hurd, Mrs. James
Hutchison, E.N., M.D.
Hutchison, Rev. S. Nye
Ingraham, George W.
Ingraham, Henry C.M.
Ingraham, Josiah P.
Jackson, W.
Jarvis, Milton B., M.D.
Jarvis, T. Newton
Jenks, Frederick
Jerome, J.H., M.D.
Judson, John E.
Kelly, Cereno
Kelsey, George A.
Kempton, Eugene
Kendall, Rev. J.L.
Lacey, Romanzo
Lambert, D.E.
Lambert, George
Lambert, John
Lathrop, George
Leonard, Hon. W.H.
Lossing, Benson J., LL.D.
Lovel, C.S.
Lovel, John
Lovel, Henry
Lovel, Thomas
Lowe, S.B.
Mallory, Edward
Marks, Cornelia Barlow
Marsh, Mary Reed
McCord, Rev. W.J.
McCue, Hon. Alexander
Mead, I.N., M.D.
Mead, J.F.
Mercereau, George
Miller, Jasper
Moore, Stoughton
Morehouse, Chauncy

Morehouse, Julius
Morgan, Henry
Morse, I.A.
Munsell, Joel
Mygatt, Abraham
Mygatt, Ambrose
Odell, S.G.
Ostrom, John
Paine, Ichabod B
Paine, Jeremiah W.
Paine, Platt
Palmer, Augustus
Parsons, O.W.
Parsons, Truman
Peck, Samuel
Pennoyer, Sylvester
Penny, Darius
Perlee, J.H.
Perry, George N.
Peters, Alfred
Peters, Henry
Pitcher, Mrs. Myra
Place, Elizabeth
Platt, John I.
Powers, Edward
Powers, F., M.D.
Powers, H.N., D.D.
Powers, P.B.
Pray, E.H.
Reed, Mrs. Betsey
Reed, C.V.A
Reed, Miss E.C.
Reed, F. Dana
Reed, Daniel, M.D.
Reed, H.V.D.
Reed, Homer H.
Reed, Horace H.
Reed, Ira
Reed, James C.
Reed, J.M.
Reed, J. Herbert
Reed, John H.
Reynolds, Hon. G.G.
Reynolds, Justus
Reynolds, Warren

Roberts, Virgil D.
Rockwell, Almira R.
Rockwell, L.E., M.D.
Rose, Harvey
Rose, Northrop
Rose, S.P.
Row, Henry
Rundall, David
Rundall, Henry
Ryan, Thomas
St. John, Dwight
Sackett, L.B.
Sayre, Rev. W.N.
Scott, C.H., Jr.
Seely, Rev. A.H.
Sedgwick, C.F.
Sedgwick, Harry
Sharpsteen, Mary Barnum
Sherman, David
Sherman, S.W.
Sherman, Shadrach
Sherman, Walter
Sisson, J.B.
Sornberger, Philander
Soule, J.B.
Smith, Albert C.
Smith, Charles
Smith, Henry W.
Smith, Myron
Smith, Richard
Snyder, William
Sprague, Col. W.G.
Stevens, Milo
Street, Chauncey
Swift, George H.
Swift, James
Swift, John
Swift, Seth
Swift, Thomas
Tallman, J.P.H.
Tanner, Jas. H.
Taylor, Henry I.
Taylor, R.B.
Terrett, Rev. W.R.
Thomson, W.H., M.D.

Thorn, J.S., M.D.
Treadwell, D.M.
Tripp, Daniel I.
Van Alstyne, Wm.
Van Dyck, Rev. L.H.
Van Dyck, H.H.
Van Dyck, Catherine C.
Walsh, Rev. J.J.
Watson, James E.
Wattles, Charles
Webster, Benjamin F.
Webster, Cynthia
Westfall, J.W.
Wheaton, Homer
Wheeler, Benson
Wheeler, B.H.
Wheeler, Burnet
Wheeler, E.E.

Wheeler, Hiram
Wiley, Allen
Wiley, Mrs. Ann M.
Wiley, J.W.
Williams, O.C.
Williamson, Geo. A.
Willson, Barak
Willson, Edward P.
Willson, Israel R.
Willson, Rev. R.E.
Willson, Samuel T.
Wiltsie, Abram
Winchell, Alex. LL.D.
Winchester, Erastus
Winchester, Milo
Winegar, Norman
Woodward, Richard

MAPS

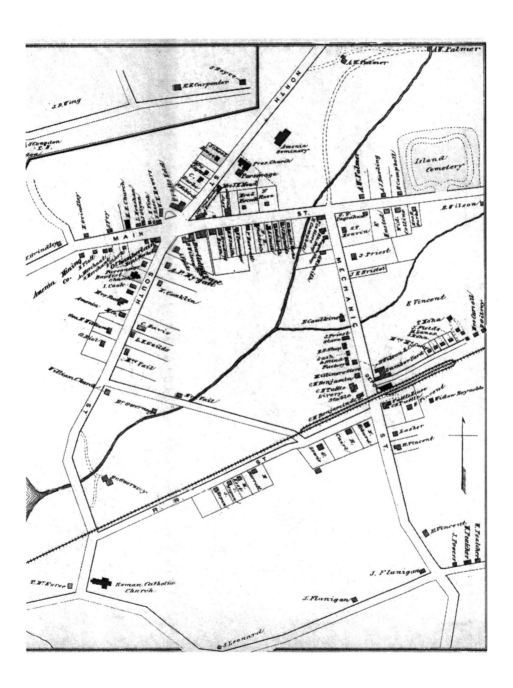

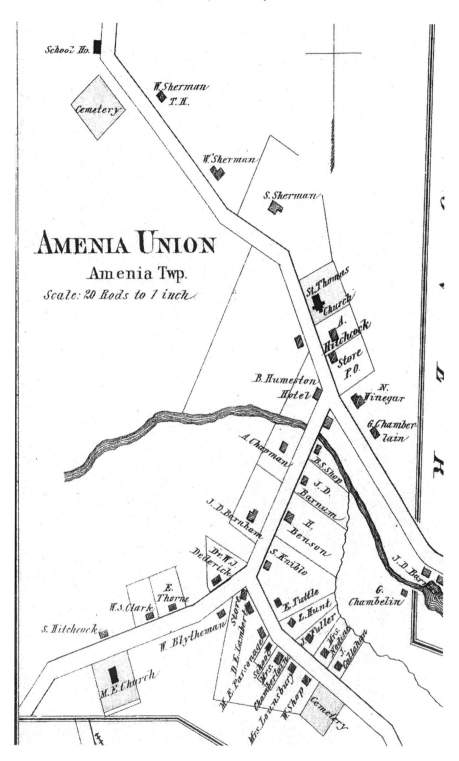

School Ho.

Cemetery

W. Sherman
T.H.

W. Sherman

S. Sherman

AMENIA UNION

Amenia Twp.

Scale: 20 Rods to 1 inch

St. Thomas
Church

A. Hitchcock
Store
P.O.

B. Humeston
Hotel

N. Vinegar

G. Chamberlain

A. Chapman

B.S. Shop

J.D. Barnum

J.D. Barnham

H. Benson

Dr. W.J. Dederick

S. Knibloe

J.D. Barn

G. Chambelin

E. Thorne

W.S. Clark

E. Tuttle

L. Hunt

S. Hitchcock

W. Blytheman

D.E. Lamberts Store

M.E. Parsonage

School
Mrs. Chamberlain

Mrs. Lodusbury

W. Shop

J. Fuller

Mrs. Nadeau

J. Callaban

Cemetery

M.E. Church

Gridley's Charcoal Pits at Wassaic (built c. 1850) *GT*

Iron Ore Mine in Amenia (c. 1870) *GT*

Amenia Railroad Station (c. 1851) *GT*

Amenia Fire Co. (established 1895) *GT*

IMPRESSIONS OF AMENIA

by

Dewey Barry

This is a compilation of articles written by Dewey Barry,

published in the pages of the Harlem Valley Times

over a period of about twelve years. (c. 1963 – 1975)

George Dewey Barry (1899 – 1977) *AHS*

GEORGE DEWEY BARRY

1899 – 1977

George Dewey Barry's grandparents, Michael and Winifred Barry, came to Amenia as Irish immigrants sometime before 1860. Dewey's parents were David P. and Margaret (Powers) Barry. His father was born in Amenia in 1862. As a young man, Mr. David P. Barry became an office employee at the local grain and lumber company of Willson & Eaton. He worked there for many years. The family lived in a lovely house on Railroad Avenue, the Barry home for almost a hundred years.

Dewey Barry grew up in the village of Amenia, attending the Immaculate Conception grade school and Amenia High School. He went on to college and returned to Amenia as a creative and skillful manager, working for more than three decades at the Willson & Eaton Company. Though a reserved and quiet man, he was an exceptional manager. He was respected by all who knew him and by those who worked with him.

Barry's love of history and his ability to write became evident with each article he contributed to the *Harlem Valley Times*. We are grateful to him for his historical essays and for the many stories, which he rediscovered and recorded for our enjoyment and for posterity. We are also endebted to Mr. McEldowney for his decision to include these "Impressions of Amenia" in the previous edition of *Early History of Amenia*.

E.C.S.
2012

THE AMENIA CHURCHES

Strong Puritan traditions were brought to this area by the people who migrated from New England to settle the land in the 1740-1750 decade. Years before the Precinct of Amenia was formed by an act of the Colonial Legislature in 1762, two church societies had been founded in the community. The Smithfield Presbyterian Church traces its origins back to 1742; while the First Presbyterian Church of Amenia derives from the Carmel in The Nine Partners organization, which was established in 1748.

Although both the Methodist and Baptist societies were established in the same century and flourished over a long period of years, neither has survived to the present time. And the crudely built meetinghouses of the eighteenth century, that served the several church denominations in their earlier years, have long since disappeared from the scene.

FIRST PRESBYTERIAN CHURCH OF AMENIA

One of the two earliest church organizations in the community was that of the Carmel In The Nine Partners which was founded in 1748 and was of Congregational denomination. In later years it was reorganized to come within the Presbyterian polity.

This society built its first church in 1758, and called it the Red Meeting House. It was located fifteen rods north of the old burying ground in the North Road section of the town, on land later owned by the Morgan family, and more recently by Dr. W.B. Lukens. Two-storied and nearly square, it was provided with galleries and square pews.

In addition to serving its own congregation, it was also shared for a number of years by the Baptists and Methodists, previous to the time when their own churches were built. During its existence, "preachers from several Protestant denominations at various times dispensed the gospel message." The famous evangelist, George Whitefield, preached there in the summer of 1770 at an outdoor meeting, which attracted a vast crowd from the surrounding countryside.

The Red Meeting House continued to serve the needs of its members until 1827 when it was finally abandoned as a house of worship. For the next six years services were held in the homes of some of the church members. Then, in 1833, the society built its church on East Main Street in the village on the site now occupied by the Amenia Theatre. It was then reorganized and brought within the Presbyterian jurisdiction and was chartered as the First Presbyterian Church of Amenia.

Some years later, the Hon. A.W. Palmer presented the organization with a gift of land on North Street on which was erected the present beautiful, stone edifice which was dedicated in June of 1867.

On October 3, 1948, the First Presbyterian Church of Amenia began the first of a four-day program of services to commemorate the Bi-Centennial anniversary of its establishment. Reverend Courtland Van Dusem was the pastor then, and participating in the services were Reverend Harry L. Reed, D.D., former president of Auburn Theological Society, and Reverend Henry Sloan Coffin, D.D., former president of Union Theological Seminary.

With an enviable record of more than two centuries of continuity, The First Presbyterian Church of Amenia remains a strong and active religious body.

METHODIST CHURCHES

The Methodists organized their Society in 1788. Their first services were held in a private home near Sharon Station. About this time several Methodist families moved to Amenia from Rhode Island and this helped to strengthen their membership. In 1808 the New York State Annual Conference was held in the Roundtop schoolhouse, on land presently occupied by the N.Y. State Division For Youth.

The Methodists erected their first church in 1812 on the property later known as the Frost estate at the corner of Route 22 and Perry's Corner Road — now the site of the Maplebrook School. In 1845 they dismantled the building and relocated their church on West Main Street in the village of Amenia. The Society flourished during the period of the existence of the Amenia Seminary, which was a Methodist institution, but it experienced a decline in its membership when the school closed in 1888, and was finally dissolved in the early years of the present century.

The building was later used as a public hall and still later as a garage. A few years ago it was damaged by fire and was subsequently demolished.

BAPTIST CHURCHES

The Baptist Society was organized in 1790, drawing some of its members from the Red Meeting House group, as well as others who had been educated in the Baptist system and who had been members of the Baptist Church at Spencers Corner, near Millerton.

Their first church was built nearly opposite the Red Meeting House on land later owned by John Haskins and probably not far distant from the present Fred P. Hoose residence on North Road. In 1851, needing larger accommodations, the society built a handsome church of colonial design on South Street in the Amenia village. The Baptist Society prospered until shortly after the turn of the century but its declining membership in later years forced its disbanment about the year 1915. The building is now occupied by the Amenia Market.

ROMAN CATHOLIC CHURCHES

In 1852 there were several Catholic families in the town and a number of Catholic men were employed in the iron ore beds at Sharon Station and Amenia. Rev. Michael Riordan of St. Peter's Church, Poughkeepsie, visited this outpost of the parish, and it was in that year that he offered the first Mass in the town, in the home of Thomas McEnroe, in the Ore Bed section of the village.

Rev. Patrick Tandy was assigned as the first resident pastor in 1868 when the first church was built. It was located south of the village, at the corner of Old Route 22 and Powder House Road. New parish lines were then drawn up, and coming within the boundaries of the Immaculate Conception Parish of Amenia were the mission churches of Millerton, Dover Plains, Pawling, Millbrook, Pine Plains and Milan.

Eighteen years later, the church was struck by lightning and destroyed by fire. In the pastorate of Rev. Daniel J. Corkery the present church was built on South Street and the parochial school was housed in its basement. The cornerstone of the new church was laid by Archbishop Michael A. Corrigan on June 12, 1887.

In 1958, a new, modern-type parochial school and convent were erected on the church premises. In April of the following year, Cardinal Francis Spellman, in his first official visit to the parish, blessed and dedicated the buildings in appropriate ceremonies, which were attended by a crowd that overflowed the new school auditorium. The late Right Rev. Msgr. John J. Kane was then pastor.

Indicative of the growth of the Catholic population in this area is the fact that all except one of the original mission churches of the Immaculate Conception Parish have since attained their own parish status. St. Patrick's Church of Millerton is the lone exception; it is a reasonable conjecture that it, too, will eventually become a separate parish.

The Immaculate Conception Parish of Amenia is one of the largest in the County outside of Poughkeepsie and Beacon, and the year 1968 will mark the first centenary of its establishment. Right Rev. Msgr. Joseph A. Dunn has been the pastor for the past several years and is assisted by Rev. Peter McKeon.

THE BETH DAVID SYNAGOGUE

One of the three present-day houses of worship in the Amenia village, is the neat, brick-structured Synagogue of the Congregation Beth David of the Jewish faith, on East Main Street. The cornerstone for this structure was laid on May 12, 1929, and several hundred people from Amenia and vixinity were present at the ceremonies.

Mr. A. H. Dube was Chairman for the occasion, and in an effective address, he "welcomed the many friends of the Jewish people who were present and extended the thanks of the Congregation for the hearty support and cooperation shown by the community in the plans of the Jews to build for themselves a place of worship and a school where their religion might be taught to the younger generation."

Rabbi Schwartz of the Vassar Temple of Poughkeepsie gave the invocation and, following with a congratulatory talk, he commented that, "a people, though small in number, when banded together for a common purpose and with the obvious cooperation of the community, could accomplish much." Other speakers included Mr. Paul A Belowitz of New York, president of the Hunt's Point Hebrew Association, Mr. Jacob Kaufman, Rev. S.W. Steele, and Supervisor Joseph B. McEnroe.

Rev. S.W. Steele, representing the religious groups of the community, said that, "every religion sends its representative to the platform to proudly share in the honors of this dedication." He noted with satisfaction the absence of intolerance among the religious elements of the town; then he read a poem, which he had written for the occasion.

The Beth David congregation has continued to prosper in the ensuing years, and, together with the church organizations of the town, remains an active force for good in the community.

THE SMITHFIELD CHURCHES

When a few log cabins were clustered around the intersection of woodland trails in the northwest corner of the town of Amenia in the 18th century, the settlement was ambitiously called the City. In the early years of the following century, one of the town's six post offices was located there, and the name was given official status. But in 1889 the post office name was changed to Smithfield.

Since the little hamlet never began to approach the size that would justify its first pretentious title, it was appropriate that it should be renamed for the church with which it became closely identified. The Smithfield Presbyterian Church traces its origins back to 1742 when the Moravian missionaries were laboring unselfishly among the Indians at Shekomeko. Tradition has it that it was their benign influence that was inspirational in the establishment by the nearby settlers of the religious society in that remote area.

The present Smithfield church structure is the third to occupy the same ground, the first of which was built in 1750. During the early years of its existence, its pulpit was supplied by itinerant ministers, as was the custom of many such rural churches of that day.

The church was one of several in the area that was visited in 1770 by the noted Rev. George Whitefield in the course of a 500-mile circuit tour. In the summer of that year, he preached under the shade of a grove of oaks, before a vast crowd that gathered from a wide area.

The earliest written records of the church begin in 1787, in this manner: "The records of the Church of Christ in the towns of Amenia, Washington and Stanford, in Dutchess County, A.D. 1787, commonly known by the name of the United Congregational Church of Christ in Westfield Society." Included in the list of names that signed to a reorganizational covenant were those of Stephen Kinney, Robert Willson and Timothy Wheeler.

A faded document dated June 5, 1809, now in possession of Gilbert Flint of Flint Hill, lists the names of thirteen men who pledged a total amount of $950 for either the repair of the first old church or for its demolition and the building of a new structure. Among the names appended thereto were those of five Thompsons, Hollister, Brown, Pugsley, Flint and Willson. In the year 1814, the first crude building was replaced by the second church to occupy the same site.

THE SEPARATE MEETING HOUSE

Another church – The Separate Meeting House – was located two miles south of Smithfield. The location is still referred to as The Separate and the road leading to it continues to be known as the Separate Road. Although no records are available to determine the exact year of its establishment, it is known that the meetinghouse itself was already standing in 1782.

It might be wondered why two houses of worship would have existed in such proximity to serve a scattered community of families in those early years. The name "Separatists," however, was that originally given to a dissident group that had withdrawn from the Church of England. Unlike the Puritans who remained in the church while hoping to reform it, the Separatisits were so dissatisfied that they worshipped apart. They did not differ in their beliefs, but rather they objected to certain of its ceremonies and practices.

The movement had gained great headway among the pilgrims and their descendants; it had its roots in that spirit of independence that had prompted them to immigrate to America. Having fled from England to escape the religious persecution, they were not disposed to accept the restraints to their freedom of worship that the civil authorities under Colonial rule continued to try to impose.

It would appear that, for a number of years at least, the Separate Meeting House had the larger following of the two churches. In the period from 1782 to 1812, it had a resident pastor of Rev. John Cornwall who also supplied the pulpit of the Smithfield Church, which in those years was without a pastor of its own.

THE SMITHFIELD PRESBYTERIAN CHURCH

When the Rev. Eli Hyde became pastor of the Smithfield Church in 1813, it was with the understanding that "all proper means be used to unite the two societies." It seems likely that this purpose was accomplished during his term, which lasted until 1821. At any rate, we hear little of the Separate organization thereafter. In 1824, the Smithfield society was reorganized and brought within the jurisdiction of the Presbyterian polity where it has since remained. The organization then became officially known as the Smithfield Presbyterian Church.

The present stately edifice was erected in 1847 under the supervision of Calvin Chamberlain and Barak Willson. Mr. Willson, an Amenia businessman, was later chosen as a ruling elder.

On October 3, 1892, the society celebrated the 150th anniversary of its founding. The occasion was marked by an address by the incumbant pastor, Rev. H.G. Birchy. By way of tradition and from written records, he traced its interesting history from its beginning – a remarkable record of continuity when it is considered that its congregation came from a widely scattered area.

It is not within the scope of this article to review the history of the various pastorates, but that of Rev. Arthur James, in more recent years, is deserving of attention. When Mr. James became pastor in 1929, the church was in a state of crisis in its affairs. The physical property was in need of restoration and there had been a marked falling off in membership. Like many of its rural counterparts, the historic old church appeared to have reached the final stages of its decline.

Enlisting the aid of old friends of the church who had thought its days were numbered, and with their loyal support and cooperation, he succeeded in reactivating the organization and giving it new strength and solidarity. After twenty-seven years as an inspiring leader and able administrator, Mr. James died in 1956, in his seventy-second year, within a day after the effective date of his retirement. To the church he left a legacy of memorable service.

In its pastoral setting, reminiscent of its pioneer origins, the Smithfield Presbyterian Church continues to serve a religious society whose traditions reach into the distant past of more than two centuries.

AMENIA'S GROWTH THROUGH THE YEARS

For nearly half a century after the issuance of the Great Nine Partners patent, this area remained only sparcely settled. It is not until the 1740-1750 decade when the land was made available for purchase in units of from two hundred to three hundred acres, at a dollar and a half an acre, that a large number of people were encourage to settle here.

In those years many families migrated from New England to take up the land that appeared it might lend itself to the successful pursuits of agriculture. Following the settlers came the tradesmen and artisans whose enterprise and skills were related to the needs of a pioneer community.

The Precinct of Amenia was formed by an act of the Colonial Legislature in 1762, and its territory was divided into three principal valleys. Included in the Precinct (and later the township) was part of the present town of North East. The name Amenia is of Latin derivation, signifying "pleasant," and was coined by Dr. Thomas Young, a resident of the Oblong.

Until well into the 19th century, the largest part of the population was in the Oblong Valley villages of Amenia Union (Hitchcock's Corner), South Amenia (Cline's Corner), and Leedsville. There were small settlements around the Steel Works and at Smithfield (the City). In the North Road section was the village of Amenia Center, which was so called because it was then the geographical center of the town. The present-day village of Amenia, which was first known as Payne's Corner and later as Ameniaville, did not begin to become settled until after the Dutchess Turnpike was built through the town in 1805.

The townships of Amenia and North East were reorganized along their present boundary lines in 1823. That part of Amenia, which had been known as North Amenia and which had a post office, was ceded to North East and its name was changed to North East Center.

The first east-west thoroughfare came from the Sharon line and followed through the Oblong Valley to the Steel Works. This was part of a main throughway from New England to the Hudson River. After General Burgoyne had surrendered his army to the American forces at Saratoga, in 1777, more than five thousand of the captured troops were marched down through this part of the country in the following year, on their way to Virginia; it was along this highway that they were conducted through the town. From the Steel Works, they continued through Mabbettsville, Little Rest, Verbank, to Fishkill.

When the Dutchess Turnpike was constructed through the town, it replaced the Oblong Valley highway as the main east-west travel route. Before the arrival of the Turnpike, the road that served this part of town came from Smithfield, across to and down to the foot of Delavergne Hill, where it turned westerly around the ore mine, thence over the hill to a point on North Street, a short distance above the site of the present Elementary School, thence through the Amenia Center village, and following a somewhat irregular course, it joined the Leedsville road at the Narrows.

The North Road village of Amenia Center had a town meeting-house and a church known as the Red Meeting House, both of which were across the road from the old burying ground. Nearby were two Protestant churches, several trade establishments, and a number of dwellings.

But as late as 1835, according to historian Joel Benton, "Leedsville was the chief point in the township," and when a site in Payne's Corner was chosen for the building of the Amenia Seminary, it came as a real surprise to the Oblong residents who had confidently expected it to be placed somewhere in their locality.

A few years later, when the New York Central Railroad Company was considering the routing of its Harlem Division through the town, arguments were advanced in favor of laying the tracks through the Oblong, with the station at Leedsville. But Ameniaville had meanwhile taken on new advantages, and when the extension was completed in 1851, it was along its present course, and the station that was built was designated as Amenia – the village then losing its appellation of Ameniaville.

About three hundred students were then enrolling annually at the Amenia Seminary where most of them were lodged. In the 1840's, a large number of workers had been imported to man the local ore mine when the product began to come into demand. This influx, together with the trade that could be expected from the farmers, encouraged the building of business places along Main and Mechanic Streets. In those years the village was experiencing a rapid growth and was beginning to take on some of its later-day appearance.

The three churches moved down from the North Road. The Amenia Times published its first issue in 1852, with Joel Benton as its editor. The First National Bank was chartered in 1864 and its banking house was located on its present site. The first Roman Catholic Church was built south of the village, in 1868. Peter Pratt purchased a small hostelry in the center of the village and in 1875 enlarged it to its present-day size. Retail stores of various types were finding a ready market for their wares. In Vail's Dutchess County Directory for the years 1870-71, of the fifty-odd commercial enterprises that were listed for the town, thirty-one of them were in the Amenia village.

Simeon Fry opened a tin shop on Main Street and was succeeded by his son, Benjamin H. Fry, who expanded the business and successfully operated an iron foundry on West Main Street. It lasted well into the present century and employed about forty men.

Barak Willson started a retail lumber and millwork business on Mechanic Street near the railroad station, which was the forerunner of Willson & Eaton Company. Among its diversified operations was a prosperous brick-making industry, which carried on until 1916. Numerous carloads of the product were shipped out in those years.

When the town's first public high school was instituted in the 1890's, it was in a wood-structured building across the road from the Presbyterian Church on North Street. Opportunity for free education at the secondary level then became available for the first time.

The Steel Works received its name from a steel manufactory which had been active during the Revolutionary War period, and around which a small settlement had grown.

When the Gridley Iron Works was started in the Deep Hollow area in 1825, it generated the growth of the village of Wassaic, so named in 1843. It was derived from "Washaick," the Indian word for the narrow valley. Noah Gridley not only gave employment to a large number of workers but also contributed much to the religious and civic life of the community.

The coming of the Harlem Division through the village, with the location of a station there, gave impetus to new business ventures. In 1861, Gail Borden established his first successful condensery, which originated the huge Borden Company. The Pendleton Millwork Company was a prosperous enterprise for a number of years. John H. Smith carried on a thriving business for the manufacture of carriages and wagons. Miles K. Lewis operated a busy Dry Goods and Grocery business.

Until the time when Borden's condensery began buying the entire output of fluid milk in the area, and before that commodity was needed in volume by New York City, it was only one of several products of the farm. The raising of sheep, hogs, and poultry, and the growing of grain, among other pursuits, had yielded more income to the farmer than did the sale of milk and butter.

But dairying began to take on more importance when it afforded the farmer a profitable income, and the production of milk has grown to be a major industry in this valley. At the present time it is probably the main contributor to the town's economy.

The town reached an apex in its population in the 1870's, but when the ore mining and iron-making industries came to their declining stages in the last years of the century, it marked the beginning of a steady descent in population, which was not reversed until the 1930's. In the early years of that depression decade, the Wassaic State School was completed, and employment became available to large numbers of people at that institution. Since that time, Amenia has seen a slow but steady increase in its population, which is now at the highest point in its history.

TRAVEL IN THE 19ᵀᴴ CENTURY

At the turn of the century, the railroad was in its heyday. A network of tracks stretched across the countryside and the few communities that did not already have the service were looking forward to the time when they could have it. The Harlen Division was completed to Chatham in 1851, but it was not until 1872 that east to west connecting lines made rail travel possible between New England and the Hudson River.

Millerton then became an important railroad center for travel in all directions. In addition to being served by the Harlem, it was the junction point of the Connecticut & Western and the Pougkeepsie & Eastern Railroads, which were the first operating lines between Hartford and Poughkeepsie.

Millerton was also the terminus of the Newburgh, Dutchess and Connnecticut Railroad, which came from Dutchess Junction (near Fishkill) up through the Clove Valley, and thence through Millbrook, Bangall, Pine Plains and Shekomeko to its destination.

Across the Connecticut border the Housatonic Railroad, in its route from Pittsfield to Bridgeport, had stations at such towns as West Cornwall, Cornwall Bridge, and Lime Rock, among others; but Sharon, surrounded on all sides by railroads, never succeeded in getting the service.

Before the emergence of the railroad, large freight hauls were made through the river and canal waterways. In 1821, a charter was obtained for the building of a canal between Sharon Valley and a point on the Hudson River, as a means of opening up this area for shipment of its farm products to the cities. An initial fund representing ten per cent of the estimate cost of the project was then subscribed by several area people and deposited with a New York City broker. But the plan miscarried when the broker failed, with a resultant loss to the investors.

Meanwhile, experimental railroads were being built in various places along the eastern seaboard, one of which was completed at Quincy, Mass., in 1823. A Poughkeepsie group then proposed a railroad to be built between their city and Sharon. But the abortive canal venture had left prospective investors in a cautious mood, and they were reluctant to take the risk at this early date.

In 1892, Sharon was still hopeful of getting railroad service. The Sharon correspondent of the Amenia Times was then chiding his readers for their impatience and bringing them up to date on the latest developments:

"Don't be in a hurry, gentlemen. Railroads are not built in a minute, and even after the first plans are drafted and agreed upon, there is still a great deal left to do. A company may say we will build the road, but that is not doing the work of surveying, building and all the other details that go to make up a fully equipped railroad service.

"The same company that controls the Central New England also controls one of the roads running into Brewster. They wish to connect the two roads, and if they do, will run the road through Sharon. They have talked of this arrangement for months, and it is not any get up of this writer when I state that there is every prospect of their doing so.

"There is still another company, independent of the above, which has had correspondence with parties in town regarding the building of a shorter line connecting, perhaps, the Central New England with the Harlem, and this would probably run through Sharon Valley. What we want is a railroad so that we can step on the cars like other people; a railroad that will lay our freight down at our feet without hauling it over Mutton Hill; and the thousand and one other conveniences that a railroad brings with it. When the time comes to help it along, lend a helping hand."

But railroad travel was not without its perils. In 1884, at Boston Corners, a terrific gale blew a southbound passenger train off the tracks of the Harlem Division. Four cars were swept down a thirty-foot embankment and only the locomotive remained on the rails. Two fatalities resulted and a number of people were seriously injured. The Amenia Times, in reporting the incident, made this caustic comment:

"The train was said to be running at a low rate of speed, but the gale was so severe that the danger was apprehended by some on board and by the conductor who got on the engine before the catastrophe happened. Two trains have been blown off the track at this place before, and it would seem that, with this knowledge, there might be inventive powers enough to prevent against future accidents of this nature."

On the occasion of the historic blizzard in March of 1888, train service on the Harlem Divisions was stalled for an entire week. Passage was blocked at Coleman's Station where a solid mass of snow was wedged between the rockcut there. On the morning of the third day after the big storm, three locomotives were dispatched to the scene with the avowed purpose of smashing through the massive drift. But after repeated assaults against the solidly packed wall of snow, one of the units was wrecked and five crewmembers met their death.

Although the railroad took over many of the functions that had been monopolized by horse, including the relegation of the tiresome old stage coach to the status of a museum piece, there were still some services beyond its range which Dobbin continued to perform. In rural areas, the same dependable steed that lent its pulling powers to a variety of farm chores, was often the same one that accommodated by carrying the family to church on Sunday; the country doctor's horse and buggy was a familiar sight in every village; and no town was without its livery stables where a horse or team with a buggy, carriage or sleigh was available for hire for the open road.

And in the posh circles of the fashionable set, the coach and four was considered the last word in genteel travel. On a September afternoon in 1890, an elegantly appointed tally-ho coach, drawn by four handsome horses, drove to Amenia from the East. The party consisted of three couples, accompanied by a manager and four uniformed grooms. They had started from Boston a week earlier for a leisurely tour of New England and had New York City as their destination. After spending the night in the hospitable atmosphere of Peter Pratt's noted hostelry, they resumed their journey toward Poughkeepsie the next morning, for an overnight stay there, before heading for New York City via the Old Post Road.

Perhaps it is just as well that the Sharon correspondent was not successful in getting the railroad for this town. The Duryea brothers were then turning out the first successful horseless carriage in America. Although considered of little significance at that time, it marked the beginning of a revolutionary change in transportation that would eventually make most of the smaller rail lines obsolete.

As for Dobbin, he was to find the horseless carriage a more formidable challenger than the iron horse had been. But the doughty old champion refused to surrender without a struggle to his newest mechanized rival. Bloody but unbowed, he was still in there battling as late as 1913.

In November of that year, Miss Nellie O'Loan's horse and rig was in collision with a Pierce Arrow at the Fountain Square in Amenia. Miss O'Loan sued the millionaire owner of the automobile for $2000, claiming that she was driving with care but that the defendant's car was being driven at an excessive rate of speed, and that, as a result, she was thrown from her wagon and had sustained bodily injuries, in addition to the damage to the vehicle.

When the case came to trial, the defense counsel contended that the real culprit was the plaintiff's horse, which he charged with being unruly and fractious. To prove his point, he stated that after the accident, the irascible animal had kicked his client in the arm.

A verdict was rewarded in favor of the plaintiff, and Miss O'Loan was awarded $450. It would not appear that the kicking incident was considered prejudicial to plaintiff's case, the jury probably having taken into account the previous good record of the accused steed and that its aberrant action might have been the result of emotional strain.

But Dobbin finally had to yield to the march of progress; then being honorably retired to pasture, it is not unlikely that he might have occasionally paused in his browsing to voice a nostalgic whinny for those good old horse-and-buggy days.

THE GREAT VAN AMBURGH CIRCUS

For many years in the 19th century, the Great Van Amburgh Circus was among the largest and most famous of the traveling, big-top extravaganzas on the American scene. In the later years of its existence, the old Amenia Fair Grounds on the North Road served as the winter quarters for the circus entourage.

Hyatt Frost, an Amenia resident, had joined the circus company in 1846, and later became its manager. In 1865, on the death of its owner, Isaac Van Amburgh, he had, with two associates, bought out the company and continued to operate it under the name of Van Amburgh & Frost Great Menagerie and Circus. Mr. Frost's estate was located at the corner of Route 22 and Perry's Corner Road – presently the site of Maplebrook School.

Isaac Van Amburgh was the first important American wild animal trainer, and was credited with the ability to "subjugate to his will and control wild and ferocious animals." After organizing his circus in the 1820's, he became internationally known as a showman and, in later years, he personally gave command performances before Queen Victoria and other members of the royalty.

His circus company went on its first annual tour as a wagon show shortly after its organization and exhibited in most cities and large towns east of Chicago, through the South and north into Canada. It probably attained the height of success in the middle years of the century but did not graduate to rail travel until 1885, after many of its competitors had made the change.

The Van Amburgh Cavalcade was announced as being the most costly and superbly attired pageant ever assembled, being composed, in addition to the other animals, of One Hundred Iron Gray Horses, besides the colossal team of the chariot. It made its grand procession through all the principal streets of the towns where it exhibited, to give the public the opportunity to witness the magnitude and splendor of its Caravan. Preceded by its Roman Chariot drawn by the "largest multiple-team in the world," it presented a magnificent spectacle. Its bandwagon was the subject of one of Currier and Ives famous lithographs, which showed the Triumphal Car passing the Astor House in New York City, in April of 1846.

Before retiring to its winter quarters on the Amenia Fair Grounds in 1881, the circus had exhibited there in October, in its last public showing of the season, before a gathering of 1800 people. The customary fanfare predceeded it; flambouyant posters distributed throughout the countryside had depicted its manifold attractions, and an advertisement in the Amenia Times had proclaimed its myriad wonders:

"The Great Consolidated Van Amburgh's Golden Menagerie and Frost's Roman Circus will exhibit at Amenia. ...Without a doubt this is the largest showing now traveling. It has been before the public for fifty years, most of which time, being under the management of Mr. Hyatt Frost. In this stupendous aggregation wil be found twenty-six cages of wild animals, birds and reptiles, comprising a rare collection of 500 living curiosities. Besides those in cages, the show has the largest Elephant in this Country, the only two-horned Rhinoceros in America, a herd of Camels, a living Nondescript, Sea Lions, an Alaskan Walrus, Giraffe, Ant-eating Bear, etc.

"The circus company is composed of over 100 of the principal equestrians, acrobats and athletes in the profession. The number of horses employed in transporting this huge institution is 212, and the number of men, women and children (including performers) is 185. The Great Van Amburgh Show has always been one of the leading institutions in this Country, and we are assured that the combined menagerie and circus this season is superior to all former ones."

But in the same year (1881), there had been some disagreement among the owners, and it was decided to sell the company assets and dissolve the partnership to permit the other two members to recover their investments. Mr. Frost then planned to reorganize the company and resume operations in the following spring.

The bizarre dispersal was held on a November day and it was considered of enough importance to attract notables of the exhibition world, including: Adam Forepaugh, representing his own famous aggregation, Lewis Sells of Sells Brothers, J.A. Bailey of Barnum, Bailey & Hutchinson Circus, as well as other lesser celebrities in the entertainment field. Reporters from the N.Y. Times and the N.Y. Sun were there, and the auction had enough show appeal in its own right to draw a large number of townspeople and farmers.

The N.Y. Times reporter began his article in the following day's issue of that newspaper as follows: "A renowned circus was under the auctioneer's hammer at Amenia yesterday. Van Amburgh's Circus, known in almost every city and hamlet east of the Mississippi, was announced to be sold piecemeal at auction, and such an extraordinary event attracted showmen from all over the Union to the little village perched at the very top of the bleak Dutchess County hills. A couple of weeks ago the circus went into winter quarters on the Amenia Fair Grounds and preparations were at once begun for the sale, which was, according to those who ought to know, the result of a disagreement among the owners."

The sale got underway in mid-morning before the large gathering; the first item, the Bactrian camel, was struck off for $625. The only two-horned rhinoceros in America, a giant weighing 3500 pounds, but quite docile, went on the block, "breathing like a blacksmith's bellows so that the auctioneen was obliged to pitch his voice an octave higher in order to be heard." In spirited bidding, the huge beast was claimed by Bailey for $2450. The elephant Bolivar, weighing over five tons and standing nine feet in height, was eagerly bid up by Sells and Forepaugh; the mammouth pachyderm was finally struck off to the latter for $7100.

Before noon a large number of the more famous of the specimens were bought by various showmen, but by nightfall some of the less spectacular of their species were still unsold. The bids on the zebra and walrus were so low that they were not sold, and these unpopular derelicts took a dim view of the entire proceedings. All the animals, whether sold or not, except the horses, were to be housed for the winter in the two large buildings then standing on the Fair Grounds.

Boxes of tinsel and trappings were bought by some of the towns-people and farmers at ridiculously low prices. Six clown suits were taken by a farmer who said his sons could wear them; a lot of Esqui-maux apparel went to a local haberdasher; but the chariots and cages were not in demand.

A week later a representative of Amenia Times visited the Fair Grounds and was shown around by Mr. Frost. Monkeys scolded, hy-enas growled and a leopard snarled, but, in general, the new inhabit-ants appeared to be as contented as possible under the circumstances. The panther was as quiet as a house kitten; four kangaroos, huddled in a pen, were apparently satisfied in their surroundings; in another pen, a Japanese hog with elephantine ears, seemed to be hitting it off quite well with his companion, a sacred cow from India; a pair of li-ons regarded the visitor with regal disdain; and a huge bear proffered a friendly hug which was politely declined. The visitor's interest was stirred by a collection of exotic birds, which included Chinese pheas-ants, paraquets and cockatoos, one pure white peacock and a noble looking ostrich. The buildings were comfortably heated and a dozen keepers were in attendance to cater to the needs of the queer assort-ment of guests.

Mr. Frost did succeed in reorganizing his company, and the annual tours continued for another eight years. Meanwhile, new specimens of the wild kingdom were imported and the circus went to rail travel.

But in that decade, significant changes of an economic nature were under way in the circus business. The better aggregations were being consolidated into larger and fewer organizations. The companies of Forepaugh and Sells Brothers joined in one such merger; Barnum & Bailey Company was combining several circuses into a single vast enterprise; and the Ringling Brothers aggregation, until then only a small mid-western tent show, was beginning its drive to outstrip all its competitors, on its way to the establishment of a giant circus empire.

This trend had its effect on the Van Ambergh operation and, in 1889, Mr. Frost liquidated the company. The Van Amburgh name, framed in circus lore, was released to Ringling Brothers who continued to use it as a sub-title for a number of years.

After a distinguished career of forty-three years as an outstanding showman, during the most romantic periods in circus history, the genial and popular Hyatt Frost retired to his estate home on the North Road, where he died in September of 1895, in his 68th year.

UTOPIAN INTERLUDE IN OLD AMENIA

"One afternoon in the early autumn of 1867, a fashionably attired Englishman arrived in the village of Amenia, New York, and inquired the
way to the Harris community. The villagers would ptobably have been
astonished had they known of the empty seat in the House of Com-
mons this man had left behind and the life he had led previously. Lawrence Oliphant had followed a long and devious route on his voyage
of self-discovery, and he had been warned as to what he must expect
at Amenia, but he did not turn back." A Prophet and A Pilgrim, by
Schneider and Lawton.

Thomas Lake Harris had founded the Brotherhood of New Life at
Wassaic in 1861. Two years later the organization purchased a farm
near the old mill south of the Amenia village, where Harris established
his first community. The fantastic career of the 19th century apostle
of Spiritualism has been the subject of numerous writings; and that of
Lawrence Oliphant is scarcely less incredible. But, unlikely as it may
seem, their bizarre story as it related to Amenia is better remembered
in far-off Japan than in the town itself.

The Harlem Valley Times, in its issue of March 28, 1968, published
a letter written by Takaski Kakuma of the Japan Broadcasting Company, which was addressed to the Mayor of Amenia. From century-
old records, Mr. Kakuma reviewed the circumstances of the presence
in the Harris community of several Japanese men, who were of the
Samurai class, and who had joined the community through the influence of Lawrence Oliphant. Mr. Kakuma also added a new and surprising aspect to the Harris story. He referred to the Japanese members as
students in the Harris Private School and credited Harris with having
made a "great contribution to the development of education in Japan."

The Community of the Brotherhood of New Life was part of a remarkable evangelical movement that emerged in the nation in the last
century, when scores of religious communal settlements, the entire
membership of which numbered in the thousands, were established
all across the land. Among the most successful of these, in the pursuit
of their religious aims, in their material accomplishments and in their
cultural contributions, were: the Shakers, the Perfectionists of Oneida,
New York, and the Mormons.

As a result of his lecture tours in England and America and his
many publications on the subject of Spiritualism, Thomas Lake

Harris was said to have had a following of more than 2000 adherents; and several hundred of the faithful were members of his communities at Brockton, New York, and Santa Rosa, California. But because of his far-out doctrines and free-wheeling practices, he was one of the most controversial religious leaders of his day. Two decades after the Brotherhood of New Life was founded, it was rent with discord, which centered around the questionable activities of its leader; this led to the defection of numbers of its members and the decline of his own influence.

Harris, as a young man, had been attracted to spiritualism. In 1848 he organized the Independent Christian Society in New York City and delivered sermons for which he claimed to have received inspiration while in trances. Among the more prominent members of his congregation was Horace Greeley.

He later joined the Mountain Cove Community of Spiritualism in Virginia, which was headed by the Rev. J. L. Scott. It was claimed that the location was the original Garden of Eden, which had remained uninhabited ever since the fall of Adam and Eve. As the principal mediums of the community, Scott and Harris presumed entire infallibility and authority as God's earthly representatives. But in spite of its idyllic setting and the promise of "escape from the vale of death," the members became disillusioned after two years, and the community was disbanded.

When the Brotherhood community first came to locate at Amenia, it consisted of about thirty adult members and a few children, among whom were several clergymen, the Japanese men, and others of both sexes from various walks of life. Two dwellings and a large farm building – adapted for the purpose – served as living quarters for most of the group.

In general, regardless of their past rank or state in life, all were required to share in the routine duties incidental to the material needs and goals of the community. In addition to the operation of a gristmill, the principal activities were the cultivation of a vineyard and the making of wine for commercial sale, the work of which was carried out under the direction of men experienced in their field. Curiously enough, this wine was not of ordinary vintage, since it was said to have been infused with an element of divine blessing, and teetotalers were piously told they might safely imbibe these sparkling waters.

It was during the course of a lecture tour in England in 1859 that Harris first met the aristocratic Lawrence Oliphant, who was then in his late thirties and a Member of Parliament. Oliphant came completely under the spell of the magnetic prophet, and both he and his mother, Lady Oliphant, were subsequently converted to his occult doctrines. When they later joined his community at Amenia, attesting to their absolute faith in Harris, they turned over to him a fortune in excess of $100,000.

Harris demanded the strict obedience of the members and he often exercised his authority in an arbitrary and capricious manner. When Lawrence Oliphant arrived in 1867 (his mother had joined the community two years earlier), the Brotherhood shepherd decreed a two-month period of probation for him. The soft and inexperienced Englishman, unused to any kind of manual work, was assigned to long hours of tiresome labor, which left him quite exhausted at the end of each day. As an added disciplinary measure, he was not permitted to socialize with the group and was made to live apart in an attic room where his meals were brought to him. All of which he patiently accepted as a necessary part of his novitiate.

It will probably come with little surprise, however, to learn that Harris left his mark on the Amenia scene, not in any way suggestive of his pretentious role in the divine plan, but rather in the more practical form of a marble-structured banking house in the center of the village, which continues to stand an an enduring monument to his business acumen.

The town's first and only federal chartered banking institution was financed and established by the Brotherhood of New Life organization. When the First National Bank of Amenia was organized in 1864, Thomas Lake Harris was elected its president. Among the directors named to serve with his were two influential and highly respected citizens of the town: Gail Borden, founder of the Borden Company, and Dr. Desault Guernsey, a prominent physician, who in later years was vice-president of the New York State Medical Association.

But the Brotherhood leader was ambitious for larger land holdings, where his community could be expanded and the winemaking industry coud be operated on a wider scale. Three years later he arranged for the purchase of more that a thousand acres near Brockton on the shore of Lake Erie, and in 1868 he disposed of the organization's investments here and moved the colony to its new location. He explained the move as being "in obedience to the direct leading of God's spirit."

The interesting sequel to this strange chapter in Amenia's history came thirteen years later, in 1881, after Harris had established his headquarters at Santa Rosa, California. Lawrence Oliphant had become disenchanted with the Brotherhood primate and, in a letter to a clergyman friend, explained his reason for breaking with him: "I severed all connections with him (Harris) because…I had reason to believe he was selling for gold and his own private ends the gifts with which God had entrusted him for the service of humanity, thus converting from a religious reformer to a religious imposter."

Oliphant sued to recover the money he and his mother had advanced to Harris and, after the adversaries had angaged in a lengthy and acrimonious airing of their differences, he finally settled for a major share of it. But the controversy led to much dissension among the members and left them divided in their loyalties.

In the later years of his life, Harris went into retirement in New York City, where he died in 1906. The number of its members having been reduced to a small hardcore of the faithful, and its communities disbanded, the Brotherhood of New Life then passed along its way, to share the fate of most of its religious communal counterparts of the 19th century.

The following sources of information are acknowledged: "American Socialisms," by John Humphrey Noyes, "A Prophet and A Pilgrim," by Herbert W. Schneider and George Lawton, Hasbrouck's "History of Dutchess County."

Immaculate Conception Catholic Church (built 1887; first edifice1868) *GT*

Beth David Synagogue (built 1929) *AHS*

Willson & Eaton Co. Yard (previously B. Willson, c.1862)
(Ducillo Construction)

Borden's Condensed Milk Company of Wassaic (est. 1861) *GT*

Pratt House and 1st National Bank of Amenia (Bank built c. 1864) *GT*

Mme. Eckle's House & Church *GT*

Amenia Seminary (1835 – 1888) *AHS*

Amenia Field Day at Troutbeck, 1914 *SHS*

OLD AMENIA INDUSTRIES

Amenia had a population of 2700 in the 1870-1880 decade, from which point it began an uninterrupted decline until the year 1930. Then resuming its upward trend, it was not until the 1950's that it again reached the peak mark of the previous century.

Contributing to the population size in the mid-19th century were the thriving industries of iron and iron ore mining at Sharon Station and Amenia; the gridley Iron Works and the Borden's Condensery at Wassaic.

IRON ORE MINING

"The iron ore of Dutchess County is very abundant and makes iron of best quality. The mines are numerous and, generally, free from water. In 1843 there were said to be ten furnaces within twelve miles of Amenia, which made in the aggregate of about 10,000 tons of iron per annum, and afforded employment to about 1,000 men as ore-diggers, coal-men, teamsters, smelters, lime-diggers, etc. Some of these were in Connecticut near the line.

"The malleable iron from the furnaces in this county (Dutchess) is highly valued for its toughness and softness, and has been extensively employed in making anchors and pistol barrels, wire, etc. The ore makes the finest car wheels and cannon, and it is said by experts to be peculiarly adapted to making the best steel." (James H. Smith's History of Dutchess County)

There were a number of ore beds in the town, the product of which was first used in nearby, small ironmaking furnaces, and later teamed to the nearest railroad points for shipment to more distant manufacturing centers. When the Harlem Division was built through Amenia and completed to Chatham in 1851, shipments were made direct by rail from Amenia and Sharon Station mines which were the largest and most productive. The Amenia mine (actually two nearby beds), west of the present village, was connected with the main line of the railroed by a spur that followed along the present-day Broadway street to a nearby railroad point.

The Johnny Cake bed was located between Amenia and Wassaic, west of the railroad. It was smaller in size but contained a good ore vein, and most of its production went to supply the Gridley Iron Works.

In the earlier years the ore bed properties were owned by local people. The Gridleys in Wassiac and the Park family of Sharon Station owned or controlled many of these properties. As the industry grew in importance, they were sold or leased to outside companies, which were better equipped to conduct the operations on the scale then required. Both the Sharon Station and Amenia mines were operated for a number of years by the Manhattan Mining Co.

The small ironmaking enterprises in the area that had had a certain measure of success in earlier years, gradually succumbed to the competition of larger eastern manufacturers and, in the later years of the century, the only remaining one of importance was the Gridley Iron Works at Wassaic.

As the Nation started to push its boundaries westward and the railroads were being built, the rich ore deposits came into demand by the steel mills and other manufacturing plants. The Amenia and Sharon Station mines then reached their highest stages of productivity and became the largest contributing factor in the economy of the town until well toward the century's close.

There was a great demand for laborers in the Country and workers were being recruited in Europe. In mid-century, millions of immigrants were arriving at American shores. Beginning in the 1840's and continuing through the following decade, more than a million Irish people came, fleeing from the hunger of the devastating famine in that impoverished country.

It was in those years that the first Irish families came in numbers to Amenia where the men had been offered employment in the ore mines. Small settlements of these families grew up around the mining points. It is estimated that upward of two hundred men were employed during the lush years of the industry.

Some of the mining companies, however, were not too sound financially and, on occasion, found it necessary to shut down operations for days at a time. In 1873, the Country experienced a severe business recession that stemmed from the failure of a large New York City banking institution. The mines were then closed for several weeks, and this caused great hardship to the workers and their families. The going wage had been a dollar a day, and there was a rumor among the Sharon Station men that work could be obtained at Ancram at 90 cents a day. Several men walked to this distant point only to have their hopes dashed when they learned that the mine there had also suspended operations.

In the 1880's it was becoming evident that the cost of deeper mining was beginning to price the local industry out of the eastern steel market. The wage level of the miners remained practically the same as it had been over the previous quarter century, while in other industries wages had increased by as much as twenty-five percent. Laborers were leaving the mines for employment on nearby farms, or were drifting to the cities. The local industry had come to a crisis in its fortunes. In the later years of that decade, the Manhattan Mining Co. found it necessary to close both its operations at Amenia and Sharon Station, and in the latter case the closing was permanent.

In 1890, a major effort was made to revive the local industry, when a group of civic-minded businessmen of the area took over the business of the Amenia mine. Modern machinery was installed, improved techniques were introduced, wages were brought in line with those of other industries, and the mine was then hopefully reactivated. In the same year, Benjamin H. Fry established a foundry on West Main Street in the village for the manufacture of sash weights. This furnished an added, though somewhat limited, market for the ore.

Meanwhile, increasing competition was being felt from Mid-Western ore developments, where the product could be gotten at nearer-to-ground levels and at correspondingly lower costs. For the next decade the company continued with some success to meet the pressure of this competition, but shortly after the turn of the century it was forced to give up its struggle. Except for a few later sporadic workings, the iron ore industry, that had contributed so much to the town's welfare for nearly a century, was defunct.

The last attempt to reactivate the mine came in 1916, during the First World War. Wagonloads of ore were teamed to the local railroad siding near the old freight station where it was reloaded into freight cars for shipment. But the venture proved to be unprofitable, and the project was abandoned after only a few carloads had been shipped out.

19TH CENTURY INDUSTRIES
THE GRIDLEY IRON WORKS

Not far off the Deep Hollow Road, near its entrance to Wassaic, can still be seen the last material evidence of a prosperous 19th century industry. There, in sheltered seclusion, are two bee-hive shaped kilns, about fifteen feet in height, constructed of flat stones that are bonded with alternate layers of concrete and still intact after more than a century.

These are the only surviving structures of the Gridley Iron Works, which was an outgrowth of a business what was established in the year 1825. A partnership, consisting of a group of townsmen, had then purchased the Johnny Cake ore bed property and began the construction of the iron works as a related enterprise. The business came into the ownership of Noah Gridley and his son, William, in 1844, and under their successful management it continued to thrive for the next forty-two years.

The physical properties of the business were located west of the Wassaic village. A large furnace was erected at the foot of the steep wooded area overlooking the village, not far from its present entrance from Route 22 (there was no highway there at that time). In the hills surrounding Deep Hollow were the charcoal burning kilns, and on the stream that runs down through those hills, a dam and a sawmill were constructed.

In the wooded section that rises to a great height, trees were felled, and moved down the slopes to the sawmill by sure-footed oxen. There the trees were sawed into four-foot lengths and carried a short distance to the kilns (of which there were then three) and stacked therein to be burned to a charcoal consistency.

In the early years, skilled colliers, who had learned their trade in Europe, were employed to supervise this highly specialized operation. Expert attention was required in this smoldering process to prevent the logs from being consumed to ashes, rather that being reduced to the needed charcoal state. Properly spaced vent holes at a four-foot height in the kiln structure could be opened or closed to control the smoldering process, depending on the prevailing weather conditions.

Each of the present standing kilns held forty-five cords of wood, and it took twenty-nine days to bring the mass of logs to the right stage of charcoal consistency. The charcoal was then used to fuel the large ironmaking furnace.

The ore was teamed from the Johnny Cake mine and mixed with other ingredients, including limestone, to form the aggregate to be heated to a malleable state in the furnace. The final operation was the shaping of the malleable iron into its end products of iron bars, plowshares and freight car wheels.

Although the entire cycle of manufacture might have been completed at this location, it appears likely that some of it was done at the Steel Works, south of the village, since this was once the center of a steelmaking establishment in the previous century. A ready market was found for the plowshares in the immediate farming area, and the other products were distributed to larger manufacturers for their own industrial requirements.

Employed in the logging, mining and manufacturing operations were about a hundred workmen. An earlier historian has observed that: "From that time (1825) the manufacture of iron and the products of the mine have contributed greatly to the common wealth of the town."

William Gridley predeceased his father in 1886, and the elder Gridley died a year later at the age of 82. Their passing signaled the demise of the business, which came to its end shortly thereafter.

That Noah Gridley was a man of business acumen is evidenced by the fact that, in addition to his ownership of the iron works, he also had financial interests in several of the ore bed properties in the area, owned thousands of acres of woodlands in Dutchess and Columbia counties, as well as much property in the village itself.

Wassaic might be said to have been built on the foundation of Mr. Gridley's wealth. Aside from the employment that his business gave to the people of the community, it was his contributions that built the Presbyterian Church in Wassaic. He also built the Wassaic Hotel (on the site now occupied by the Maxon Mills feed plant). And, it was because of his financial assistance that Gail Borden was able to establish his very successful condensery in the village.

The old furnace has long since disappeared from the scene. Only a crumbled mass of stone and concrete remains to mark the site of the mill dam which has given way to the pressure of flooding waters. The hills of Deep Hollow that once hummed with the activity of busy workmen have lapsed into the serenity of their pristine setting.

19ᵀᴴ CENTURY INDUSTRIES
BORDEN'S CONDENSERY

The giant Borden Company, largest in the dairy products field, and widely diversified in other industries, has its successful beginning in a modest wooden building in Wassaic.

It was there, in 1861, that Gail Borden established his business for the manufacture of his condensed milk product, the patent for which process he had obtained five years earlier. Mr. Borden, then in his sixty-first year, had come to the crossroads of a somewhat checkered career and had spent much time in experimenting in the concentration of solid and liquid foods.

Two previous attempts to launch his new enterprise had met with failure. First, at Torrington, Conn., in 1857, a nation-wide business depression had caused him to discontinue operations. A subsequent venture at Burrville, Conn., came to its end in 1860, because of disagreements with the plant owners, together with the disappointing results of trying to market his product. Indeed, the consuming public was only mildly interested in his new food concept and still preferred the health-giving beverage in its natural form.

Undiscouraged by these reverses, he looked for a more favorable environment in which to locate his plant, and was attracted to the Harlem Valley by its fertile pastures, which appeared to be particularly suited to dairy farming. And so great was his faith in his product that he had no doubt of his eventual need for a large supply of milk. But his more immediate need was for capital, and, in his predicament, it was not surprising that he should seek assistance from one of the Valley's wealthiest businessmen in the person of Noah Gridley of Wassaic.

Mr. Gridley agreed to invest in his project to the extent of a piece of land and a building on the west side of the railroad at the Wassaic station. With additional support from Jeremiah Millbank, a prominent financier of the day, Mr. Borden was able to purchase the necessary complicated machinery to begin operations. A corporation was organized in the name of the New York Condensed Milk Company (later changed to the Borden Company).

It was in the same year that the armies of the North and South were engaging in the opening hostilities of the Civil War, and the alert inventor was successful in contracting with the U.S. government to supply the Union armies with his milk product. This proved to be the turning point in his fortune. For the next three years his greatest problem was to meet the demands of his government commitments.

By the year 1863, the condensery was taking the entire milk output from the farmers within a fifteen-mile radius and turning out fourteen thousand quarts of its product daily. In order to keep up with the increasing demand, it was necessary to tap new sources of milk supply. New plants were built at York, Pa., at Livermore Falls, Maine, and in 1864, at Brewster, N.Y., the largest one of all.

The condensery's need for a large volume of milk marked the beginning of a significant change in the farm operations in the entire area. Up to that time, dairying had been only one (and not the most important) of a diversity of agricultural activities, which also included the growing of grain for market, the raising of sheep, hogs and poultry, and various other pursuits of husbandry. Now, an assured and profitable market was established for the sale of milk, and, normally, there was no restriction on the amount to be supplied. This has resulted in the growth of the dairy industry over the years, to its present size in the northern Harlem Valley and the eastern Dutchess area, which today is one of the richest milk producing sections in the nation.

In the later years of the century, when New York City found it necessary to reach out farther for its fluid milk requirements, receiving plants were built (not only by Borden's, but by its competitors, also) at nearly every railroad point in the dairy farming section. It then became more economical for Borden's to move some of its manufacturing to its Mid-Western plants and to employ part of its Wassaic facilities for shipment of fluid milk to the City.

About 1890, the first Wassaic building was replaced by a larger and more modern one that was better designed to meet the demands of the Company's expanding markets. Then, in the 1920's, the manufacturing phase was discontinued entirely at Wassaic and the plant was used exclusively for the receiving and shipment of fluid milk. In this period, about 50,000 quarts were being shipped out daily. During the lush years of the plant's existence, between seventy-five and one hundred people were steadily employed, including about twenty-five women.

Railroads eventually lost the business of transporting the milk, when the trucking companies began this service direct from the farm. This has resulted in the closing of all the old milk receiving plants, which once gave great employment to a large number of workers in many small towns.

When the Borden Company closed its operations at Wassaic, about twenty-five years ago, it made a gift of the property to the town of Amenia. In recent years, the building has been occupied and enlarged by the Tri-Wall Container Corporaton, which has continued to employ a large number of people in the community.

Gail Borden died in 1874, but as a memorial to his ingenuity, his name lives on in the company that he established more than a century ago.

THE STORY OF LIZZIE ST. JOHN AND HER RISE FROM THE GHETTO

"That woodland scene that lies in front of my cottage door, appeared to me, that Sunday morning, like a vast altar dressed by the hand of the Creator. The long-wished-for hour came, and I began to mount the hill to the church with a joy that the human heart seldom knows." – Lizzie St. John Eckel.

The time was July 21, 1872. It was the occasion of the dedication of St. Genevieve's Chapel. The small church, of French provincial design, gracefully crowned the hilltop that looked down upon a valley of pastoral charm.

The narrow dirt road that ascends from South Amenia to the top of Clark Hill on the Connecticut side of Amenia Union was suddenly alive with horse-and-buggy traffic on that summer Sunday, more than a century ago. The crowd that was gathering to take part in the celebration of the opening services included a delegation of priests, religious and notables of the laity, who had arrived from New York City.

It was a day of triumph in the career of a beautiful and ambitious woman, who, as a child, had lived with her poor relatives in South Amenia. Her mother was the notorious Maria Monk, who years earlier, had claimed to be a fugitive from the Convent of the Black Nuns of Montreal. The publication of her book, purporting to be an exposé of that institution, had its overtones in a wave of anti-Catholicism in that period, which was climaxed by the burning and desecration of several convents in eastern cities.

Lizzie St. John was the daughter of that misguided woman. At the time of her birth, March 17, 1838, in a squalid tenement in New York City, her mother was already in the shadow of alcoholic addiction; her dissolute father, the black sheep of an otherwise respectable family, was reaping the bitter fruit of a misspent life; the fourth member of that wretched home was three-year-old Georgina, the daughter of Lizzie's mother by a former liason and the adopted daughter of Mr. St. John.

When Lizzie was six years old, a son was born to her parents, but within the next year, her mother had reached such a state of incompetency that her father took the children and placed them in a boarding house in the City, after which she never saw her mother again. A year later, Mr. St. John brought the children to South Amenia to live with certain of his relatives with whom he was still on good terms.

Shunted between three such homes, Lizzie lived with her relatives for the next seven years. Although she was provided with all her material needs and given the benefit of the customary education of that day, her life in the country was not a picture of the joys of carefree youth; her happiest hours were spent in roaming the hills of the Oblong, where she learned to "fall in love with nature."

For, having been deprived of the love that is the lot of normal childhood, left to her own resources in the city slum streets and made to carry the stigma of her parents' sins, she had been instilled with feelings of insecurity and troubled emotions. In trying to impose on her the yoke of discipline to which she was unused, her guardians failed to realize her need for a corresponding measure of affection, and denied this softening influence, she reacted perversely with impish pranks around the home and in the neighborhood. The failure to find a common ground of understanding resulted in a growing estrangement and finally a complete alienation between her stern guardians and their rebellious young ward.

So, it came as a matter of relief to all concerned, when, as a blooming lass of fifteen, she decided to break the ties that had held her to her country relatives and launch her career in the city of her birth. Her sister, Georgina, had already left home to work in New York.

Recounting her early struggles to earn an honest livelihood during the next two years of lonely existence, she wrote: "I began then to learn, more than before, of the darker and more revolting side of the tragedy of life, and I found, alas, that what is vile and selfish, and cruel can be disguised under the sacred name of love and friendship."

But along with the darker aspects of city life, she also found that it was not without its warmer and sympathetic side. In her loneliness, she was befriended by the Mother Superior of the Academy of the Sacred Heart. Later, a Judge and his wife became her benefactors and took her into their home to live. They sent her as a boarding student to the Monson Academy of Massachusetts, where she took full advantage of her educational opportunities, and, advancing to the more select Madame Martinet Academy in Manhattan, she responded readily to its refining influences.

She was married at the age of nineteen, in a Methodist parsonage, to Samuel Eckel, a government employee. The following January, she accompanied her husband to Washington, where, in her own words, "I entered into its intrigues and frivolities with a zest and earnestness of which only a giddy mind, filled with vanity and self-love, is capable. It was in Washington society that I first learned of the magical power of woman over man, and even over the destinies of the state."

It is hardly surprising that the discovery of such knowledge proved to be heady wine for one who, only a few short years before, had been a scorned little country girl.

The couple's first child was born in May 1861 and survived only a few months. But after the first rapturous years, they found themselves drifting apart and had already separated in October 1862, when their second daughter was born. Mrs. Eckel and her child were living in New York the following January, when she received the news of her husband's death in Washington.

The following summer she again felt the call of adventure, and she sailed for France with her daughter. Fortified with letters of introduction, she was admitted to the sophisticated circles of Parisian society, where, for several years, in the company of members of titled nobility and the diplomatic set, she basked in its sensual pleasures. "I had Machiavelli as my breviary and had no doubt that its maxims pointed the way to happiness." She was courted by many, but the one she loved, a Viscount possessed of titles, wealth and position, although not aloof to her charms, could not quite bring himself to the point of marriage, which left her unhappy but not discouraged.

She had been influenced by the writings of Voltaire and was skeptical of all religions. One suspects, then, that her conversion to Catholicism was motivated less as a result of any strong convictions than because she hoped it might please the Viscount. At any rate, it seemed to have had a chastening effect, and she professed to be surfeited with the shallowness of society life. Returning to New York in the summer of 1868, she made a religious retreat and fancied that she was inspired by divine revelations.

On the occasion of a visit to Amenia in 1869, she returned to a favorite haunt atop of Clark Hill in Amenia Union, where she had roamed as a child. Now, an earlier dream to have a church built in these hills took form in her imagination. She had then thought, "It is just the place in which to worship God." She arranged for the purchase of a piece of land on this lovely site and scarcely noticed that it was located over the border in Connecticut.

Her relations with the Viscount having now ended, she was absorbed in religious mysticism. But she received little engouragement in her ambition to build her church. She talked with Father Tandy, the pastor of the Immaculate Conception Church of Amenia, but he was not convinced of the need for another church within so short a distance and referred her to Archbishop McCloskey of New York.

The latter was not enthusiastic, and the matter was further complicated because the property was in Connecticut and outside his jurisdiction. But the resolute Madam persuaded him to request the Bishop of Hartford to authorize the transfer of the property to the New York archdiocese, to which the Connecticut prelate readily agreed. At this point, however, the Archbishop, allowing his better judgment to prevail, decided he could not conscientiously continue to lend his support to the scheme and he tactfully informed Mrs. Eckel of his decision.

Although disappointed at this turn of events, the visionary lady, believing that her authority was ordained by a higher power, was not to be deterred by mundane considerations. The old house on her Clark Hill property had been remodeled for her own use, but the funds for the church were not forthcoming in the required amounts, and it became necessary to negotiate a bank loan to complete the construction. She did, however, receive many costly gifts to furnish the chapel, including a chalice from Tiffany's, an original painting of St. Genevieve by the artist Carter, altar linens and other expensive furnishings from various sources.

Madam Eckel's moment of glory finally came on that day when St. Genevieve's chapel was officially opened for services. Although denied the sanction of diocesan recognition, it was graced by the presence of two Jesuit priests, Fathers Bapst and McDonnell, various members of religious orders, a distinguished organist and vocalist from St. Xavier's Church in New York, and prominent members of the laity.

Indeed, she could scarcely have hoped for a more enthusiastic reception for her dream project. At the second Mass the church was filled with worshippers from the surrounding area; and the afternoon Vesper services attracted people of other denominations in addition to those of her own faith. The Amenia Times gave this glowing report in its next issue:

"This beautiful Catholic chapel, erected by Mrs. St. John Eckel, opened on Sunday, the 21st inst. The edifice is placed upon a lofty and commanding eminence, and the propect to the south and west is of great extent and striking beauty. The temple itself is a model of good taste and artistic excellence, while the decorations of the interior are exceptional, even to the most fastidious criticism. The windows are of the choicest designs and of exquisite workmanship, while the altarpiece, representing the Savior and St. Genevieve, is a painting so charming that the gazer upon its sweet outlines cannot refrain from the thought, "a thing of beauty is a joy forever."

"The sermon was delivered by the Rev. Father Bapst of the Order of Jesuits, and it was a clear and eloquent exposition of the cardinal doctrines of the Catholic Church. At five o'clock p.m., the chapel was opened for the beautiful vespers, and again the sweet music peculiar to these evening devotions was given the most charming effect. The service concluded with an excellent sermon by the Rev. Father McDonnell, and all who attended both services could not but have been pleased with what they saw and heard of the ritual and worship."

Many of the people who had come from New York remained during the next few days. On Wednesday evening, another priest, Father Merrick, addressed a large congregation. But with the departure of the priests and the last visitors, an ominous stillness settled over the lofty but remote chapel, the site of which would seem to have been better suited to a cloistered monastery than to a house of worship that could only hope to draw a sufficient number of Catholics to warrant the holding of regular services.

Mrs. Eckel's hopes for the future success of her venture were further dimmed when her bankers began pressing for the repayment of the loan. And the final awakening came, when in trying to meet the obligation, her resources were strained to the point of impoverishment and she was obliged to appeal to her friends for financial assistance. During the next year, she and her daughter lived on the charity of her friends in New York.

She was living in her home in Amenia Union in 1874, when her autobiography, "Maria Monk's Daughter", was published, and from the proceeds of its sale she was able to repay her creditors and recoup part of her own losses. It was a candid chronicle of her life story, and in it, she repudiated the statements made by her mother in the latter's earlier volume of so-called disclosures. The discredited author of the book had, however, later admitted that the account was fraudulent and that she had written it to make money.

In May 1875, while still living in her country villa, Mrs. Eckel and her daughter narrowly escaped with their lives, when a fire of unknown origin broke out in the night and destroyed her home. Such cruel blows of fortune might have discouraged a less indomitable spirit, but if she was impractical she was not unresourceful. Two years later, and still under forty years of age, she had met and married S.B. Harper, who was said to be a member of the prominent family of publishers.

Little is known of the remaining years of her life, which were spent in seclusion, away from the public eye. The news of her death in Rome, in 1917, was briefly reported in a New York City newspaper. Her only known survivor was her daughter, Mary Eckel, who was then a member of a religious order.

The lonesome chapel, abandoned and left to deteriorate, was further stripped by vandals, and at last disappeared in flames at the hands of mischievous roisters in 1894. But the remarkable story of Lizzie St. John continues to live in the folklore of the Oblong.

THE AMENIA SEMINARY

On the site now occupied by the Elementary School on North Street in the village of Amenia, once stood the Amenia Seminary. At the time of its completion it consisted of three buildings, four stories high; and it flourished as a famous seat of learning for fifty-three years, from 1835 to 1888.

It was the first of such academies in the State and among the first in the country to successfully operate on a co-educational basis. During its existence, students were enrolled from every state in the Union, as well as from South America, and many of its faculty and alumni later attained positions of prominence in the fields of business and other professions.

This was during the time when the public school system was limited to the lower grades and when education beyond that level was available only at such schools as the Seminary. Only a minority of families of that day could afford the luxury of an education that would be comparable to the high school standards of a later period. And, although most of the students came from families of varying degrees of affluence, for others it was at the expense of some sacrifice.

Although a number of such schools existed, particularly in the east, there is much evidence to support the claim that the Seminary ranked with the best of these. – "The Amenia Seminary then gave such preparation for college as was equaled by few schools in the land." Indeed, it merited attention in the ninth edition of the Encyclopedia Britannica.

When the slow and tedious methods of travel and communication of that time are considered, it is somewhat remarkable that an institution of this kind, located as it was in a small and rather remote village (without even a railroad until 1851), should have attracted students from such great distances. The fact that it did attests to its high academic standards.

In 1832 the community became enthusiastic on the subject of education and resolved to have a seminary located somewhere in the town. The village of Amenia was then known as Ameniaville or Payne's Corners. There was a difference of opinion among the leaders as to the most suitable location and one such, in the village of Leedsville in the township, was favored by many. However, after two years of discussion and planning, the site then known as Cook's Hill on North Street was chosen.

The five following paragraphs are excerpts quoted from an article on the subject by the late Joel Benton and published in 1907. Mr. Benton was a native of Amenia, a former student of the Seminary and an historian of some renown.

"The Amenia seminary was established in 1835 by a group of sagacious men of the Methodist faith. Prominent among them were the Powers, Ingraham and Hunt families, with others to assist them, nearly all of whom reside in Amenia. This was sixteen years before the village in which it was placed had a railroad, the Harlem extension not being completed to Chatham Four Corners until the summer of 1851.

"The village itself was called Payne's Corners. Some debate was had, in fact, on the propriety of choosing this site, as Leedsville was the chief point in the township of Amenia, which had six post offices and which once had much of the Town of North East as a part of its territory, with a post office called North Amenia.

"The school, when it started, consisted of a middle building and two-thirds of the north building nearest thereto. In 1841, or there abouts, the south building was added; and in 1848 the north building was extended. The three buildings must have been originally eighty feet in length, and the extended north one must not be far from one hundred feet long. They are about four stories high. It became the first academy in the State.

"The Seminary taught all branches in the college curriculum, as well as music and art. It had a library of 1,600 volumes and on one of the catalogues of about forty years ago (about 1866) there is a record of 247 students.

"When there was a United States Literature Fund at Albany for the distribution of money to those seminaries and academies that taught certain branches (the distribution to be pro-rata), the Amenia Seminary would have $1000 of it, some similars schools in other counties $700, and so on, in a descending ratio, to the one at the foot of the list."

The Seminary was also somewhat of a pioneer in another way. The idea of co-education was generally frowned upon by people of that time, but, again quoting Mr. Benton, "the greatest thing, however, which this seminary did (not, however, without some hesitation and doubt) was to prove the success of its perilous experiment. It certainly carried through, to eminent success, a co-educational scheme, which gave the girls as good a chance for a liberal education as it gave their brothers." For a few years, for which we have the registration records, the ratio of males to females ran rather consistently about two to one. In the year 1853, a total enrollment of 364 students is recorded.

Under the constitution of the school corporation, it was provided that the principal must be a Methodist minister. "But it was not agressively sectarian and the teaching body were among the most urbane and cultured people that could anywhere be found." That the governing body and faculty members were, in general, persons of character and intellectual stature is evidenced by the fact that many of them subsequently became distinguished in the areas of religion and education.

A few of these are cited as follows: two chancellors of Syracuse University, three presidents of Weslyan University, two presidents of Northwestern University, one president of Michigan State University, one president of Caflin University of South Carolina and four Methodist bishops.

Among its more notable alumni were: Honorable B. Platt Carpenter, a governor of Montana; J.P.H. Tallman, a surrogate of Dutchess County; John Curry, a judge of the Supreme Court of California; Miles T. Granger, a judge of the Superior Court of Connecticut; Gilbert Dean, a member of Congress; and Judson S. Landon, an associate justice of the Court of Appeals of New York State.

Numbered among its students were hundreds who were the ancestors of many present day residents of Dutchess County, as well as surrounding counties. In an article of this length, it would be impractical to list them all, but it is likely that in the records of some of the older families might be found the name of a forebearer who was once enrolled at the Seminary.

From the eighteenth annual catalogue for 1853, we learn that the curriculum consisted of Departments of English, Mathematics, Natural Science, Moral Science, Belles-Lettres, Ancient and Modern Languages. Additional courses in Drawing, painting, and Music were also available to those who wished them.

The tuition per term for each of the above courses ranged in price from $2.00 to $10.00. The charge for board was $30.00 per term. And from another source we learn that the average annual salary of a professor was $300.00 to $400.00, including board. Obviously, the purchasing power of a dollar was greater than it is today and, of course, our standard of living is on a much higher plane.

Among its by-laws were a few of interest and which were in contrast to certain current attitudes:

"All students are expected to cherish a respectful deference for the authority of the faculty, and to exhibit, at all times, a gentlemanly and lady-like deportment.

"Smoking in any part of the building, playing at games of chance, using profane or indecent language in the Seminary, or elsewhere, are totally forbidden.

"The two sexes will not associate together in walking or riding, nor stand conversing in the halls or public rooms, but when necessary, they will ask the Principal the privilege of seeing the person they desire.

"A strict observance of the Christian Sabbath will be required: no unnecessary noise will be allowed, nor may any on the day roam in the fields, nor frequent the village, nor collect at each others' rooms or engage in any of the ordinary weekday diversions. All are required to attend public service at such place as their parents or guardians may direct, unless excused by some one of the officers of the institution."

In the year 1856 there appeared the first issue of the "Lightning Bug," a four-sheet paper, to be published semi-monthly, which described itself as an independent literary publication of the Philomatheon Society of the Amenia Seminary. A careful perusal of its first four issues evinced only articles of an abstract nature, which would be of little interest to a later generation.

However, it did include a few advertisements and, appearing among the literary compositons expressive of the lofty aspirations of its young contributors, was one, which disclosed ambitions of a more mundane, albeit unusual, nature on the part of the author. Since it is revealing of its time, it is deserving of republication.

MATRIMONIAL

A lady, who considers herself to possess all desirable qualities of mind and heart, takes the present opportunity to announce to the public in general, and all eligible young men in particular, that she is still unmarried, and has no objection to entering into a matrimonial engagement with any person who possesses the following qualities, viz: He must be of an obliging disposition, not use tobacco in any form, be able to read and write, and to possess an income of not less than $2000 perannun. The lady in question declines to give her age, assuring the interested public, however, that she is not under fifteen, nor over forty. Any person wishing to enter into correspondence with this lady may address S.L.M., Amenia Seminary.

With the advent of the public high schools, which were beginning to be provided by the more progressive communities in the latter half of the century, schools of the type of the Amenia Seminary became unnecessary and in 1888, it closed its doors after a remarkable career.

Eighteen years later, in 1906, some of the old students arranged for a reunion of the alumni. On August 22nd of that year, more than two hundred of these assembled at the school grounds, among whom were several who had enrolled when the Seminary was first established. "Fully a thousand people gathered to celebrate the occasion," including friends, relatives, and prominent citizens of the surrounding area.

The formal program for the afternoon and evening sessions was carried out in a festive atmosphere and consisted of addresses by some of its more famous alumni and faculty members, together with musical interludes by a well-known orchestra. The evening session drew to its close on a farewell note as the old group joined in chorus to the strains of "Auld Lang Syne," and thus did the Amenia Seminary pass into history.

Since we have borrowed rather freely from Mr. Benton in compiling this article, it is fitting that it be concluded with his poetic tribute to lovely Amenia:

"Amenia, Amenia, thou classical garden,
More famous and fair than Calypso of old."

THE AMENIA FIELD DAY

What was so unusual about the Amenia Field Day, which was an annual event in the years 1910 through 1914, that it inspired laudatory editorials in such prominent and far-flung periodicals as the Chicago Evening Post, The Country Gentleman, Collier's Weekly and La Follette's Magazine, among others; was acclaimed by many of the nation's leaders; and received the cordial endorsement of a former president of the United States?

Certainly, the rural field day was not an uncommon affair in the community life of the period. For many years, the old Fair Grounds on North Road had been the scene of many such festivals, when townspeople and farmers from the surrounding countryside would gather for a day of recreation.

To answer the question, it is, perhaps, necessary to examine the background of the person who originated the Amenia Field Day. J.E.Spingarn had been a professor of Comparative Literature at Columbia University in the early years of the century, had achieved distinction as a literary critic, and had several scholarly publications to his credit. Attracted by its natural beauty, he had purchased the "Troutbeck" estate at Leedsville a few years earlier, and having resigned his position at Columbia University in 1911, came there with his family to live.

Nestled in its tranquil setting of rustic charm, "Troutbeck" had been in possession of the lettered Benton family for generations. By reason of the family's association with Emerson, Thoreau and John Burroughs, it had acquired a literary tradition all its own. Burroughs had described it as "the loveliest farm in America," and the gifted Sinclair Lewis, who was a friend of Mr. Spingarn, had once called it "a grass-grown cathedral." It is not surprising that it should have particular appeal for the scholar and nature lover.

But he had not resigned a full-time position to assume the easy life of a country gentleman. In addition to his literary work, to which he could now devote more time, he had a diversity of interests, not the least of which was his love for horticulture, to which pursuits the fertile fields of Troutbeck were well adapted. And so well did he develop his experiments in the culture of plants and shrubs, as well as becoming an authority on the vine clematis, that he established Troutbeck as a "Mecca for horticulturalists the world over, who made regular pilgrimages to it."

He was a staunch crusader for the rights of the underprivileged, and one of the first presidents of the N.A.A.C.P. His liberal ideas brought him into close association with Theodore Roosevelt, and although not personally ambitious for political office, he stumped vigorously for the Progressive Party candidate in the presidential campaign of 1912.

Nor did the importance of these activities keep him aloof from those of a more parochial nature. Urbane and unassuming in his manner, he settled easily into the community life and was well received by the townspeople. Taking a lively interest in the affairs and problems of the community, he assumed an active role and asserted a quite leadership in many of its civic and social endeavors.

Charles E. Benton wrote of Spingarn: "It is not strange that he helped to bring new ideals into this community's life. The former social life of the farm population had largely disappeared, except what was preserved by the granges. The fairs and cattle shows had succumbed to their own abuses, and under these conditions, he conceived the idea that the community, to be well-knit in its community life, must cooperate in its amusements, as well as in its work, for play is a necessary part of modern life and as important to the welfare of the rising generation as "organized play" or "cooperative recreation."

"With this thought, he founded Amenia Field day, a day for public enjoyment, which should be free of gamblers and fakers; a countryside day of free and wholesome recreation, managed by the whole community and free for all.

"It was held at Troutbeck in a broad level of perfectly dry ground in the intervale meadow, and from the first meeting in 1910, the annual gathering has been a marked success, attracting wide attention not only throughout the county but in the country at large. 'Indeed, I do believe most cordially in the Amenia Field Day, and it is just the kind of thing that ought to be done,' wrote Theodore Roosevelt."

When the idea was proposed to the town leaders, it met with their ready response and approval. Proceeding in its organization, committees were formed, and more than a hundred of the townspeople eagerly enrolled in the work of its preparation. In a fine spirit of cooperation, nothing was left undone to make the affair a pleasurable one for all.

In an era when country life was more exacting in its demands for all but the landed gentry, the pleasures of the rural populace were limited, and the field day afforded one of the few opportunities for escape from the humdrum workday, when the people would come together in a holiday atmosphere of recreation. And because the first Amenia Field Day seemed to offer something beyond the customary pattern of such festivals, it attracted more than the ordinary interest outside the immediate borders of the community.

On that August day in 1910, they came from up and down the Harlem Valley by train to Amenia, from where they were transported in open, horse-drawn wagons over the unpaved, dusty road to the fair ground; from the same conventional means they arrived from nearby towns and beyond; a few automobiles, earlier-day heralds of the motor age, were driven to the scene by their prosperous owners, stirring up billowing dust clouds en route, and forcing nervous steeds to give ground at their roaring approach; village boys, astir with the thrill of adventure, strode sportively over the three-mile course; and when all were assembled at the Troutbeck meadow, they numbered to about three thousand.

Beginning mid-morning with a ten-mile parade "around the mountain," with prizes for the most beautifully decorated floats, wagons and other vehicles, the program covered a whole gamut of activities and attractions designed to encourage the participation of many.

In addition to the customary athletic sports, with classes for all who might wish to compete, and including those suitable for the female sex, there were also the free-for-all contests of old-fashioned football, tug-of-war and ball relay, trap shooting and other contests of skill.

Interspersed among these more competitive games, were the colorful folk dances, gracefully performed by well rehearsed groups of young people; play festivals, and an historical pageant staged on the banks of the picturesque Troutbeck pond; and for the pleasure of those whose taste inclined to the social dances, a pavillion had been erected and an orchestra provided.

In those years, *sans* television and radio, the country folk enjoyed the privilege of hearing a public speaker of some prominence, and from the prairie state of Nebraska had come U.S. Senator Moses Clapp for the purpose; nor did that visiting dignitary disappoint as he proceeded to deliver an appropriate address in the best traditions of the oratorical style of the day.

Of more practical interest to the farmers were the agricultural features, and on proud exhibit throughout the day were the prize products of the farm. Particularly interesting was the introduction by Farm Bureau agronomists of a new forage crop, alfalfa, which in the following years has proven to be one of the most important forage grasses in the area.

No field day in those years would have been complete without its baseball game at a time in the nation's history, when the sport had a special allure for the people, comparable, perhaps, to that which the famed Olympic games had for the ancient Greeks. And not until the last exciting play at six o"clock did the tired but happy gathering disperse, to wend its way homeward or to proceed to the village for the final attraction of the day's program – the evening band concert at the public square.

Whether or not the concepts of community recreation were fulfilled in their application to the Amenia Field Day, there is no doubt that the affair itself was successful in its popular appeal, as attested by the spirit of festive gaiety that animated the crowd. Each succeeding year saw an increase in attendance, and in 1913, it numbered ten thousand people.

The Hudson, N.Y. Republican, in a July issue of that year, commented: "What was formerly called the Amenia Experiment now deserves a new name. It is no longer an Experiment. In 1910, this alert and alive village undertook to have a free field day. The result was a wholesome gathering of wholesome people in the number of three thousand; the next year a more elaborate program was carried out and five thousand people attended. Last year eight thousand people were there and the program was the best yet. As a result of this progressiveness, this pretty Dutchess County village has had more free advertising than any place of its size in the country."

In that year, it was reorganized and incorporated in the name of the Amenia Field Day Association with a board of thirty directors, residents of Amenia and neighboring towns, to administer its affairs. As it gained national prominence, it was referred to as the Amenia Idea and similar celebrations were inaugurated in various parts of the country. In addition to the influence it exerted through the press, the Association was constantly receiving requests for information in regard to its work from every section of the Union and was cooperating with various organizations in spreading the idea of community play.

The Youth's Companion said of it: "The characteristic that distinguishes the Amenia Field Day and that makes it worthy of imitation in every country community is the spirit of neighborliness and the wholesale enjoyment that lies behind the movement – the attempt through community cooperation to make country life more attractive socially for old and young alike." And a governor of New Hampshire wrote: "Your successful accomplishments in establishing rural recreation has aroused my interest and admiration."

Coinciding within days of the last Amenia Field Day in 1914, the guns of August had signaled the outbreak of the First World War. None could then foresee all its tragic consequences, or the upheaval of change that would follow in its aftermath. The Field Day was suspended for the war's duration, but when the great conflict finally came to its end four years later, many of the older patterns of country life had been swept away.

The rural field day was geared to the leisurely pace of the horse and buggy, and like its contemporary, having served a community need in a more provincial age, made its quiet exit from the changing scene of history.

THE END

RECENT PUBLICATIONS
RELATED TO AMENIA HISTORY

Amenia, N Y – A Baseball Town, Celebrating Amenia's Baseball Heritage, Webutuck Country Schoolhouse Assoc., 2007

A History of the South Amenia Presbyterian Church, Ruth Barlow, 1959, 2nd Edition, 2009

A Year in the Life: The Daily Journal of Edward Dean, An Amenia Union Farmer, Julian Strauss and the After School Boys Club, 2009

"Fountain Square," compiled by Gary Thompson, newspaper articles and photos, Amenia Historical Society, 2010

From the Kitchens of Amenia, A Cookbook Celebrating 300 Hundred Years, Amenia Historical Society, 2004

Harlem Valley Pathways through Pawling, Dover, Amenia, North East, and Pine Plains, Joyce C. McGhee and Joan Spence, Arcadia Publishing, Charleston, SC, 1998

"Lake Amenia New York," a reprinted booklet about the Lake Amenia Resort, photos and captions, United Development Corp., NYC (c.1950)

Memoirs of A Farm Boy, Marvin Van Benschoten, 2011

Memories from a Country Schoolhouse, John Quinn, Webutuck Country Schoolhouse Assoc., 2008

The History and Records of the First Presbyterian Church, Amenia, New York, 1748 – 1910, edited by Brian Cook, 1997

Vital records of the following Churches: First Presbyterian Church of Amenia, Smithfield Presbyterian Church, South Amenia Presbyterian Church, Gridley Chapel of Wassaic, and St. Thomas Episcopal Church of Amenia Union, transcribed and indexed by Arthur C.M. Kelly, Kinship Books, Rhinebeck, 2004 – 2011.

DISCARD

DISCARD

CPSIA information can be obtained at www.ICGtesting.com
Printed in the USA
BVOW021634030712

294315BV00003B/1/P